外贸口语逆袭

50 种商务场景
秒变谈判高手

毅冰◎著

中国海关出版社有限公司

中国·北京

图书在版编目（CIP）数据

外贸口语逆袭：50 种商务场景秒变谈判高手 / 毅冰
著 . -- 北京：中国海关出版社有限公司，2025.
ISBN 978-7-5175-0901-1

Ⅰ . F75

中国国家版本馆 CIP 数据核字第 2025BT5476 号

外贸口语逆袭——50 种商务场景秒变谈判高手

WAIMAO KOUYU NIXI —— 50 ZHONG SHANGWU CHANGJING MIAOBIAN TANPAN GAOSHOU

作　　者：毅　冰
责任编辑：夏淑婷
责任印制：孙　倩
出版发行：中国海关 出版社有限公司
社　　址：北京市朝阳区东四环南路甲 1 号　　　　邮政编码：100023
编 辑 部：01065194242-7539（电话）
发 行 部：01065194221/4238/4246/5127（电话）
社办书店：01065195616（电话）
　　　　　https://weidian.com/? userid=319526934（网址）
印　　刷：北京利丰雅高长城印刷有限公司　　　　经　　销：新华书店
开　　本：710mm×1000mm　1/16
印　　张：12.75　　　　　　　　　　　　　　　　字　　数：175 千字
版　　次：2025 年 6 月第 1 版
印　　次：2025 年 6 月第 1 次印刷
书　　号：ISBN 978-7-5175-0901-1
定　　价：65.00 元

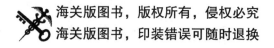

自 序

　　将时光回退到 2012 年。我在写《毅冰私房英语书——七天秀出外贸口语》(简称《七天秀出外贸口语》) 这本书的时候，在想些什么呢？

　　那时候的我，工作刚进入第八年，就职于香港利丰集团，正是踌躇满志的阶段，有好多想表达的东西，有好多行之有效的方法和技巧，迫不及待地想分享和传递给大家。

　　在那个年代，外贸人学习的渠道很窄，能够获取信息和内容的地方非常有限。从论坛的帖子到一本本书的出版，就是我跟大家对话的方式。

　　在那个年代，并没有所谓的商业模式，也不存在什么变现路径，能够支撑我长期更新内容、答疑、一本本书写下去的动力，就只有纯粹的喜欢。

　　在那个年代，做好外贸需要学习很多的知识，来实现和同行的差异化。要有业务技能和开发技巧，于是我写了《外贸高手客户成交技巧》；要能把邮件写得专业简洁，像外企员工那样自然，于是我写了《十天搞定外贸函电》；要能给客户打电话、和客户见面交流，摒弃畏惧心理，于是我写了《七天秀出外贸口语》。

我相信，这一系列的书籍，包括后面的《外贸经理人的 MBA》和《外贸创业 1.0》等十多本书，都是按照外贸人真正的需求，用自己的经历和经验，一点一点用心打磨出来的内容，也的确影响了一代又一代的外贸人。

《七天秀出外贸口语》的出版，是因为我想写一本给外贸新人和初学者的案头书，一本真正意义上可以应用和落地在外贸行业的实用工具书。之所以用七天做内容，灵感来源于美剧的紧凑，把外贸环节所对应的不同场景做浓缩，让新入行的朋友们可以迅速入门，能够第一时间跟客户开启交流的通道，作为邮件背后的补充。

当你有紧急事情要跟客户打个电话

当你有一些情况通过文字说不明白

当你在展会上直面客户和现场沟通

当你接待客户走访工厂和具体介绍

当你陪同客户用餐和其他私人安排

…………

都不免需要用到英语口语，总不能完全靠面部表情和肢体语言，或者随时随地都安排一个翻译人员在身边吧？

所以当年的《七天秀出外贸口语》，真的影响了几代外贸人，成了很多人长期翻阅找素材的案头书，或用来培训公司新人的工具书。

既然如此，如今为什么要让这本书消失呢？为什么要用一本全新的书来替代呢？

别急，听我细细道来。核心就是以下三个原因。

第一，当年的纸张、印刷、版面和封面设计，是严重落后于如今的审美。别说读者们，就连我自己，都实在看不下去了。

第二，那个年代主要还是使用光盘，可如今还有谁的电脑里带着光驱？不至于因为某一本书还要买个那个年代的移动光驱吧。

第三，过去的内容，某种程度上已经落后于如今的外贸发展，我们不能抱残守缺，用十多年前的口语书来应对如今的工作。

所以，旧书的改写就变得迫在眉睫。拖延症的我，拖了一年又一年，拖到出版社还在一次次加印，读者还在一次次买单，拖到我自己都看不下去了，都不好意思了，只得抽出时间，正儿八经开始启动口语书的改写工作。

然而改写的过程，让我发现了新的问题。

为什么要改写？为什么不索性写一本全新的口语书？反正都要花时间，逐字逐句去改，去调整内容，那为何不跳出固有的窠臼，难道还要受限于当年的框架和格局吗？难道今时今日的我，还不能打败十几年前的我吗？

自然是能打败的！而且如今外贸人的需求，跟那个年代也不可同日而语，需求不知道高了多少倍。

如今缺口语书吗？不缺。缺商务英语的视频或者各种自媒体的学习资料吗？也不缺。那缺什么？缺真正落地、真正写给外贸人的实战型口语书。更缺能够渗透到业务环节本身，不局限于电话和当面交流，而把外贸人的谈判技巧和业务能力渗透进去的商务英语类书籍。

这些，不正是我的强项吗？让大家学的不仅是一个英语口语的语言技能，而且是用口语来开展业务工作，用口语来进入外贸谈判！一念至此，我果断决定调整内容，重写，所有案例重新做，所有内容推翻重来，直接以"口语谈判"为主线，来构建用词、句型、案例，调整这些模块，重塑外贸类口语书的标准。

我相信这一本书的问世，能够继续引领外贸英语口语这个细分行业，打破我当年保持的纪录。

下笔千言，此刻尽无言。

希望这本献给外贸人的新书，能呈现一个不一样的毅冰。

这里凝聚的，是自己这二十年外贸路的点滴，是"路漫漫其修远兮，吾将上下而求索"的勤力，是"千磨万击还坚劲，任尔东西南北风"的追求。

忆惊喜雀跃，叹心酸落泪，看西湖月满，听东浙潮来。

愿你在人生的每个阶段，都有奔赴山海的热情，都有一往无前的动力。

你在进步。

我也是。

毅冰

2024 年 10 月 17 日

于上海静安

目 录

第六章

面对突发状况，娴熟传递价值的核心表达

第七章

更多金句表达，让你随时随地拿出来使用

打破沟通障碍，
英语紧急电话的
独门技能

1 报价后的电话跟进技巧，用起来

故事背景

> 毅冰在中国香港展会上认识了一位美国客户 Bob，当时客户询问了一款太阳能灯的价格。毅冰当晚就写邮件给客户，提供了报价单。展会结束后很久，客户迟迟没有回复，写了邮件跟进，依然石沉大海。于是，毅冰决定直接打电话过去，了解一下具体情况。

Dialogue:

Yibing: Hi Bob, this is Yibing calling from ABC Trading in China. <u>How's it going</u>?

Bob: Hey Yibing, I'm good. How about yourself?

Yibing: I'm doing well, thanks! I wanted to <u>follow up on</u> the email I sent you last week regarding the solar lights pricing. Did you have a chance to <u>take a look</u>?

Bob: Oh, I just got back from a business trip. I haven't checked my emails yet, but I'll definitely go through it and <u>get back to you</u> ASAP.

Yibing: Great, appreciate that! If you have any questions or need further details, feel free to <u>shoot me an email</u> or give me a call.

Bob: Absolutely, Yibing. Will do.

参考译文 📖

毅冰：嗨，Bob，我是来自中国 ABC 贸易公司的毅冰。最近好吗？

Bob：嘿，毅冰，我还不赖。你呢？

毅冰：我也很好，谢谢！我想跟进一下上周我发给你的关于太阳能灯价格的邮件。你有机会看吗？

Bob：哦，我刚出差回来。还没看邮件，但我肯定会尽快看一下然后回复你。

毅冰：太好了，十分感谢！如果你有任何问题或需要更多细节，请随时给我发邮件或打电话联系我。

Bob：当然，毅冰。会的。

Words & Phrases（词汇和句型）

How's it going? 你最近好吗？（类似于 How are you doing?）

follow up on something 跟进某个项目

take a look 看一下

get back to you 回复你（相当于 come back to you 或 reply you）

shoot me an email 发我邮件（这里的 shoot 比 send 更加有力，侧重于发送的动作）

Chinglish Correction（中式英语纠错）

如果运气好，你明天就能收到报价单。

【Chinglish】

If you're lucky, you could receive the offer sheet tomorrow.

【Native English】

Please the pigs, I will let you receive the offer sheet tomorrow.

▶ **毅冰补充：**

这里，please the pigs 是一个地道的口语表达，表示"如果运气好""如果够走运""如果一切如愿"……这个句子的本质和内涵，是供应商要加油，提高工作效率，迅速解决问题，尽量让客户第二天就收到报价单，跟客户是否感兴趣毫无关系。

所以千万不能用 somebody be lucky 这个词组，可以换一个地道的短语替代。

2 催促紧急事宜，电话要这样打

故事背景

> 毅冰和 Bob 经过一个多月的辛苦谈判，终于拿下了一个 20 尺柜的订单，确认好订单细节，也收到了客户的定金。但样品寄出后，迟迟没有收到 Bob 的正式书面回复。毅冰心急如焚，又不敢自作主张安排大货生产，这一耽搁就拖延了整整两周时间。现在，毅冰需要跟客户紧急打电话确认一下，看有没有遗漏的问题，能否进入大货生产。

Dialogue:

Yibing: Hi, could I speak with Bob, please?

Carol: I'm afraid Bob's currently on a business trip in Las Vegas. May I ask who's calling?

Yibing: Sure, this is Yibing from China. I'm following up on the solar light sample. It's quite urgent, and I need his <u>approval</u> to proceed with <u>mass production</u>.

Carol: Hi Yibing, I'm Carol, the Merchandise Planner here, and I <u>work closely with Bob</u>. He's been checking his emails while he's away, so I'd recommend sending him a message. I'm sure he'll get back to you soon.

Yibing: Thanks, Carol! Actually, I've already sent him a few emails, but I haven't heard anything yet. Do you happen to know when he'll be back?

Carol: He's expected back by next Monday, but I can't confirm the exact time.

Yibing: Got it. I'll try <u>reaching out</u> to him again on Monday. Thanks so much for your help, Carol. It was great speaking with you!

Carol: <u>You're welcome</u>, Yibing! Feel free to reach out if you need anything else. Take care!

参考译文 📖

毅冰： 嗨，请问我可以和 Bob 通话吗？

Carol： 抱歉，Bob 目前正在拉斯维加斯出差。请问您是哪位？

毅冰： 我是来自中国的毅冰。我想跟进一下太阳能灯样品的情况。这件事很紧急，我需要他的批准才能安排大货生产。

Carol： 你好，毅冰。我是 Carol，是这里负责订单和采购计划的专员，我和 Bob 一起工作。他在出差期间一直都会查收邮件，所以我建议你给他发个邮件。我相信他会很快回复你的。

毅冰： 谢谢你，Carol！其实我已经发了几封邮件给他，但还没有收到回复。你知道他什么时候会回来吗？

Carol： 他预计下周一回来，但我不能确定具体时间。

毅冰： 明白了。我下周一再试着联系他。非常感谢你的帮助，Carol！

很高兴跟你聊天!

    Carol: 不客气,毅冰!如果你还需要其他帮助,随时联系我。保重!

Words & Phrases(词汇和句型)

approval 确认、批准

mass production 大货生产、批量生产

work closely with somebody 和某人共事

reach out 联系、沟通(比 contact 更加口语化)

You're welcome! 不客气,不用谢。

Chinglish Correction(中式英语纠错)

价格跟包装方式和数量有关。

【Chinglish】

The price is related to the packaging and quantity.

【Native English】

The price depends on the packaging and quantity.

▶ **毅冰补充:**

"depends on" 这个短语,虽然常常翻译成"依靠",但也有"取决于""跟……有关"之意。而 be related to 是"联系""联结""关系到"的意思,用在这里并不是特别恰当和到位。

3 接到客户的 Cold Call（陌生来电），这样应对

故事背景

毅冰从展会回来两个月了，这天下午突然接到一个电话，是一个德国客户打来的。他在网上看到毅冰所在公司的联系方式，现在打电话咨询几款产品的信息。对方的语速很快，又带有一些口音，英文不是太好懂。

Dialogue:

Nina: Hi, is this Yibing?

Yibing: Yes, speaking.

Nina: Hi Yibing, this is Nina calling from Germany. I got your contact information from your <u>official website</u> and wanted to inquire about the pricing for your <u>lawn lamps</u>.

Yibing: Lawn lamps? Could you please provide the item numbers?

Nina: Sure. The item numbers are BM-2365, BM-2399, and BM-2386. Also, if you could recommend some of your <u>best-selling models</u> for Western and Central Europe, that would be great. I'd like to discuss them with <u>local retailers</u> here.

Yibing: Sorry, could you repeat the last one? BM-2365, BM-2399, and...?

Nina: BM-2386.

Yibing: Got it. I'll prepare the quotes and send them over via email. Could you please share your email address with me?

Nina: No need, I'll send an email to the address listed on your website. Just reply to that when you've got the information.

Yibing: Sorry, what was that?

Nina: I'll send you an email, and you can reply to me once you've prepared the quotes.

Yibing: Sounds good. No problem!

参考译文 📖

Nina：你好，请问是毅冰吗？

毅冰：是的，我就是。

Nina：你好，毅冰，我是从德国打来的 Nina。我从你们官网上找到了你的联系方式，想咨询一下草坪灯的价格。

毅冰：草坪灯？你能提供一下产品编号吗？

Nina：当然，产品编号是 BM-2365、BM-2399 和 BM-2386。另外，如果你能推荐一些在西欧和中欧热销的款式，那就更好了。我打算和本地零售商谈谈。

毅冰：不好意思，你能再重复一下最后一个产品编号吗？BM-2365、BM-2399 和……？

Nina：BM-2386。

毅冰：明白了。我会准备报价单并通过邮件发送给你。能告诉我你的邮箱地址吗？

Nina：不用担心，我会发邮件到你们网站上显示的邮箱。收到后请回复我就行。

毅冰：抱歉，你刚说什么？

Nina：我会发邮件给你，你准备好报价回复我就可以了。

毅冰：好的。没问题！

Words & Phrases（词汇和句型）

official website 官方网站

lawn lamp 草坪灯

best-selling models 热销产品

local retailers 本地零售商

Sounds good. 好的。

Chinglish Correction（中式英语纠错）

我们会在 12 月 15 日以后收到样品。

【Chinglish】

We will receive the sample after the 15th of December.

【Native English】

We won't get the sample back until the 15th of December.

▶ **毅冰补充：**

"not...until..." 这个句型，在英语口语中十分常见。加上它，整个句子就显得更加灵动，不那么死板。又如：He did not realize how much he loved his hometown until he moved abroad.（直到搬到国外，他才意识到自己有多么热爱家乡。）

4 接老客户电话，不要过于死板

故事背景

> 毅冰接到一个老客户 Thomas 的电话，针对某款产品要下返单。但是时间非常紧迫，15 天就要交货，而价格也是不小的问题。客户需要按照去年的成交价来执行，而今年原材料价格上涨幅度非常大，毅冰十分为难。

Dialogue:

Yibing: Hi Thomas, how's going?

Thomas: Hey Yibing, <u>all good</u>. Got some news that'll make your day.

Yibing: Oh yeah? Let's hear it!

Thomas: I'm putting in another order—one full 40 feet container. But here's the catch: you've got to <u>get it done</u> in 2 weeks.

Yibing: Wow, that's going to be a real stretch for us. Can you give us 25 days instead?

Thomas: Unfortunately, no. We need to ship it in 20 days to meet the <u>promotion schedule</u>.

Yibing: Alright, let me talk to the team and figure out the timeline. I'll get back to you with the price and delivery details.

Thomas: Come on, Yibing, let's not <u>mess with the price again</u>. Keep it the same as last time, okay?

Yibing: I hear you, but you know with labor costs going up and all these supply issues, it's getting tougher...

Thomas: Yeah, I get it. But <u>bottom line</u>—what matters most is locking in the order, right? I can't risk haggling with my customer. We can eat into our margins a bit, but we've got to keep the client happy. Just think it over and confirm today, alright?

Yibing: Okay, I'll run it by my boss and get back to you ASAP.

Thomas: Awesome. Thanks, Yibing!

参考译文 📖

毅冰： 嗨，Thomas，最近怎么样？

Thomas： 嘿，毅冰，一切都不错。我有个好消息，绝对让你开心。

毅冰： 哦？快说说！

Thomas： 我准备再下一个订单，一个 40 尺的整柜。不过有个条件，你们得在两周内完成。

毅冰： 哇，这对我们来说可有点难啊。能不能给我们 25 天的时间？

Thomas： 抱歉，不行啊。我们必须在 20 天内发货才能赶上促销。

毅冰： 好吧，我先和团队商量一下，看看时间安排。我会尽快给你报价和交货细节。

Thomas： 别这样，毅冰，咱别再折腾价格了。就按上次的价格来，好吗？

毅冰： 我明白，但你也知道，现在人工成本上涨，再加上供应链的问题，确实挺难的……

Thomas： 是，我明白。但是，最重要的还是确保订单，对吧？我不能冒着和客户讨价还价的风险。我们可以少赚点，但得让客户满意。你考虑一下，今天给我确认，好吗？

毅冰： 好的，我跟老板商量一下，尽快回复你。

Thomas： 太棒了，谢了，毅冰。

Words & Phrases（词汇和句型）

all good 挺好的（口语化的表达，用来表示各方面都不错）

get it done 完成、搞定、解决

promotion schedule 促销计划

mess with the price again 再谈价格（这里的 mess，更侧重于"拉锯"）

bottom line 底线（往往在谈判中表示最终的红线）

Chinglish Correction（中式英语纠错）

明年四月的广交会什么时候开始？

【Chinglish】

When will the Canton Fair begin in April next year?

【Native English】

Could you please find out when the Canton Fair will be held in April next year?

▶ 毅冰补充：

短语 find out 有"查明"的意思，加上 could 和 please 这类用词，让整个句子表达上显得更加委婉。Canton Fair 是传统意义上的"广交会"的英文翻译。官方正式英文名称为 China Import & Export Fair（中国进出口商品交易会）。

5 初次开发潜在客户，如何防止被挂电话

故事背景

> 毅冰在网上找到一家澳大利亚公司，他们从事园林灯具相关的生意。可网站上找了好久，并没有相关联系人的邮箱，只有几乎无效的在线填写表单。又尝试通过 LinkedIn（领英）搜索，也没有找到这家公司的联系人或其他更多信息。于是，只能打电话过去问问，看能不能联系到相关的买手或负责人。

Dialogue:

Brenda: Hello, who's calling?

Yibing: Hi, this is Yibing from ABC Trading in China. We supply solar lights and other outdoor lighting products. Could you put me through to your purchasing team, or whoever looks after imports?

Brenda: Oh, you're calling from China? We already get <u>a fair bit of stuff</u> from China.

Yibing: Yes, I understand. But I'd love the chance to show you our new range. Everything is up to <u>SAA standards</u> for Australia and New Zealand.

Brenda: <u>Righto</u>... How about you <u>flick me an email</u> with some details on your company and products? Maybe recommend a few with your <u>sharpest pricing</u>. We'll have a look, and if it's all good, I'll pass it on to the buyer.

Yibing: That sounds perfect, thanks so much! Could I have the chance to grab your email address?

Brenda: Sure thing, it's BrendaMiller1212@xxx.com. Oh, and it's Brenda, by the way.

Yibing: Got it. Thanks heaps, Brenda! Great chatting with you.

参考译文 📖

Brenda：你好，请问是哪位？

毅冰： 嗨，我是来自中国 ABC 贸易公司的毅冰。我们提供太阳能灯和其他户外照明产品。你能帮我转接到采购部门，或者负责进口业务的买手那里吗？

Brenda：哦，你是从中国打来的？我们已经从中国进口不少东西了。

毅冰： 是的，我知道。不过我很想有机会向你展示我们的新产品。我们所有产品都符合澳大利亚和新西兰的 SAA 标准。

Brenda：好的……你可以给我发一封邮件，介绍一下你们公司和产品吗？顺便推荐几个价格最有竞争力的款式。我们会看一下，如果一切都没问题，我会把相关资料转给买手。

毅冰： 听起来很不错，非常感谢！我有机会得到你的邮箱地址吗？

Brenda：当然，邮箱是 BrendaMiller1212@xxx.com。顺便说一下，我的名字是 Brenda。

毅冰： 明白了。谢谢你，Brenda！很高兴和你聊天。

Words & Phrases（词汇和句型）

a fair bit of stuff 相当多的东西（a fair bit 是口语化表达，表示数量很大）

SAA Standards 澳大利亚电器安全标准（SAA 是 Standards Association of Australia 的简称，SAA 标准除了澳大利亚本土，也适用于新西兰市场）

righto 好的、没问题（常见于澳大利亚人之间的口语表达）

flick me an email 给我发邮件（澳大利亚口语中常见的表达）

sharpest pricing 最有竞争力的价格

Chinglish Correction（中式英语纠错）

昨天报给你的价格是错的。我会尽快发你新的报价单。

【Chinglish】

The offer sheet which I sent you yesterday was wrong. I will send you the new one soon.

【Native English】

I quoted you the wrong price. I'll fix the offer sheet and update you soon.

▶ 毅冰补充：

这里的动词是 fix，表示"调整""修正"，这意味着原来的报价单里，其实大部分资料是正确的，只有一小部分需要修正。而 update 表示"更新"，是可以用作动词出现的。当然了，updated offer sheet，则是"更新后的报价单"。

6 邮件后的电话跟进，SOP（标准作业流程）用起来

故事背景

毅冰收到一个新客户 James 的询盘，当天就报了价格，但等了一周后都没有任何回复。于是再跟进一封邮件，又等了一个礼拜，依然石

沉大海、杳无音信。毅冰想电话跟进一下，看看究竟是什么原因。是产品问题呢，还是价格问题？还是有什么别的不知道的情况？

Dialogue:

Yibing: Hey, <u>is James around</u>?

James: Yeah, this is James.

Yibing: Hi James, this is Yibing from China. I sent you the quotes about two weeks ago, but I haven't heard back yet. Did you get my emails?

James: <u>Which company are you with again?</u>

Yibing: I'm with ABC Trading, based in Shanghai.

James: Oh, right! I did get your offer and <u>passed it along</u> to my assistant. She's <u>been swamped with checking</u> all the details and will get back to you before the weekend.

Yibing: Got it. Sorry for the <u>follow-up</u>, James!

James: No worries at all. Have a great day!

参考译文 📖

毅冰： 嗨，James 在吗？

James： 是的，我就是 James。

毅冰： 你好，James，我是来自中国的毅冰。我大约两周前给你发了报价单，但至今没有收到回复。你收到我的邮件了吗？

James： 请问你是哪家公司的？

毅冰： 我是来自上海的 ABC 贸易公司。

James： 哦，明白了！我收到了你的报价单，并且已经转给我的助理了。她现在正忙着核对所有细节，预计会在周末之前给你回复。

　　毅冰：明白了。不好意思打扰你了，James!

　　James：没关系。祝你有个愉快的一天!

Words & Phrases（词汇和句型）

Is James around? 请问 James 在吗?（这里 around 更加口语化，更具随意性）

Which company are you with again? 请问你是哪家公司的?（这里的 again 是一种礼貌用词，表示我好像知道，但需要再确认一下）

pass it along 传递、转交

be swamped with something 被某事淹没（表示十分繁忙）

follow-up 跟进

Chinglish Correction（中式英语纠错）

现在进展如何?

【Chinglish】

What is the status now?

【Native English】

What is the current status?

▶　**毅冰补充：**

　　在英语中，now 这个词更加侧重于正在进行的动作，而不是一种状态。而这里，询问如今的进展，current status 更加契合语境，也是商务英语中常用的一种固定搭配。

7 邮箱有问题，如何紧急告知客户

故事背景 🖉

　　毅冰的邮箱最近出了点问题，给一个法国老客户 Reno 写邮件老是被退信，但是给别的客户写邮件，又都一切正常。为了不让工作受到影响，只能暂时用别的邮箱来联系 Reno。为了避免误会产生，除了写邮件正式通知外，毅冰还给 Reno 专门打电话告知了一下。Reno 是法国人，毅冰不免用法语寒暄几句，然后用英文说正题。

Dialogue:

Reno: Bonjour! Comment ça va aujourd'hui?

Yibing: Bonjour, Monsieur! This is Yibing from ABC Trading.

Reno: Hi Yibing! Great to hear from you again! It's been a while. How have you been?

Yibing: Not too bad. Just really swamped since the Canton Fair. And you?

Reno: I'm good. Just got back from a family vacation.

Yibing: Oh, where did you go?

Reno: We went to Monte Carlo in Monaco.

Yibing: That sounds fantastic! Must have been a great trip!

Reno: It really was.

Yibing: By the way, I'm having some trouble with my email server. I just sent you a message from my personal email. Please use that for now until my work email is back up.

Reno: No problem, I'll check it and get back to you.

参考译文 📖

Reno：（法语）你好！今天怎么样？

毅冰：（法语）你好，先生！（英语）我是来自 ABC 贸易公司的毅冰。

Reno： 你好，毅冰！很高兴再次听到你的声音！有段时间没联系了。你最近怎么样？

毅冰： 还不错。自从广交会之后特别忙。你呢？

Reno： 我很好。刚和家人度假回来。

毅冰： 哦，去了哪里？

Reno： 我们去了摩纳哥的蒙特卡洛。

毅冰： 听起来太棒了！一定是一次很棒的旅行！

Reno： 的确是。

毅冰： 对了，我的邮件服务器出了点问题。我刚刚用我的个人邮箱给你发了一封邮件。在我的工作邮箱恢复正常前，请通过这个邮箱联系我。

Reno： 没问题，我会查看并尽快回复你。

Words & Phrases（词汇和句型）

Not too bad. 还不错，还不赖。

family vacation 家庭旅行

Monte Carlo 蒙特卡洛（摩纳哥核心城市）

email server 邮件服务器

back up 恢复

Chinglish Correction（中式英语纠错）

样品费是可以退还的。

【Chinglish】

The sample cost could be returned.

【Native English】

The sample charge could be refunded.

▶ **毅冰补充：**

样品费，虽然根据上下文表达，也会出现 sample cost 这样的用词，但是在商务英语中，真正地道的表达，就是使用 sample charge，它的出现频率极高。而"费用退还"，并不是 return，而是 refund，表示"退款"的意思。全额退款，就是 full refund。issue a full refund，是"发起全额退款"。

接待展会客户，事先准备的口语秘籍

8 新客户走进摊位，要使用参照物锚点

故事背景

在香港贸易发展局举办的礼品展上，两个客户经过毅冰的摊位，停下脚步打量了一下架子上陈列着的产品，然后讨论起来。过一会便走上前，把行李放到一边仔细挑选。对话就在这样的情况下发生了……

Dialogue:

Yibing: Hi there! Welcome! Feel free to <u>take a look around</u>.

Customer A: What's the price on this one?

Yibing: Which one are you asking about? The colorful piece?

Customer A: Yeah, that's the one.

Yibing: Ah, that's one of our newest designs. It's $3.50 per piece, with a minimum order of 3000 units.

Customer A: That's <u>a bit pricey</u>!

Yibing: (smiling) I understand. It's a new arrival, and the quality speaks for itself. Plus, this is one of our hottest designs for the season. But I'm sure we can work something out. Are you looking for a <u>long-term partnership</u>?

Customer A: Well, it depends on the pricing. We usually get something similar for a little less.

Yibing: I see. If you're considering a larger order <u>down the road</u>, we might be able to discuss a discount for future purchases. But for the first order, we're offering a trial with 500 or 1000 units to help you test the market. Does that sound fair?

Customer A: Hmm, that could work. What about shipping costs? Are they included in this price?

Yibing: Shipping isn't included in the unit price, but we work with reliable logistics partners to ensure competitive rates. If you'd like, I can get a shipping quote to the <u>destination port</u> based on your preferred delivery time.

Customer A: OK, that would be helpful. We need it within three weeks—can you manage that?

Yibing: For 500 or 1000 units, we can certainly meet that timeline. If you decide to place a larger order later, we'll need to confirm availability with our production team. But three weeks for this batch is no problem.

Customer A: I'll have to run it by my team. Price is still a concern though, especially with shipping on top.

Yibing: I completely understand. What I can do is follow up with a detailed offer, including the shipping costs, and see if we can offer a small discount for your initial order. How does that sound?

Customer B: That sounds reasonable. We'll take a look at everything once we have the full details.

Yibing: Great! I'll send you the revised offer today, along with the shipping quote, and I'll make sure we include a couple of samples in the shipment as well.

Customer A: Perfect. Could you send the samples to the address on this card?

Yibing: Absolutely. I'll follow up by email and confirm all the details. Thank you both for stopping by!

Customer B: Thanks, Yibing. We'll be in touch soon.
Yibing: Looking forward to it! Have a great day!

参考译文 📖

毅冰： 你们好！欢迎光临！请随意看看。

客户 A： 这个多少钱？

毅冰： 你指的是哪个？是这个彩色的吗？

客户 A： 对，没错。

毅冰： 啊，这是我们的新款设计。每个价格是 3.5 美元，最小订量是 3000 件。

客户 A： 有点贵啊！

毅冰：（微笑）我理解。这是新款，并且品质很好。这个是我们本季最热销的设计之一。不过我相信我们可以谈谈。你们考虑长期合作吗？

客户 A： 嗯，这取决于价格。我们通常会拿到价格低一些的类似产品。

毅冰： 我明白。如果你们未来考虑大批量订购，我们可以在之后的订单上讨论折扣。但对于首次订单，我们可以提供 500 或 1000 件的试单，让你们测试市场。你觉得这样合理吗？

客户 A： 嗯，这样可以考虑。那运费呢？是包含在这个价格里吗？

毅冰： 运费不包含在单价里，但我们有可靠的物流合作伙伴，可以确保有竞争力的运价。如果你们需要，我可以根据你们的交货时间给你一个运费报价，发货到你指定的目的港。

客户 A： 好的，那会有帮助。我们需要在三周内收到货——你们能做到吗？

毅冰： 对于 500 或 1000 件来说，三周内没问题。如果之后你们决定下更大的订单，我们需要跟生产团队确认一下货期。但这批货三周内肯定没问题。

　　客户 A：我得和我的团队商量一下。价格还是个问题，特别是加上运费。

　　毅冰：我完全理解。我可以给你发一份包含运费的详细报价，并且看看我们能否在首次订单上提供一个小折扣。你觉得这个方案怎么样？

　　客户 B：听起来不错。我们会在看到所有细节后再做决定。

　　毅冰：太好了！今天我会把修订后的报价和运费一起发给你们，还会确保样品也包含在发货里。

　　客户 A：完美。你可以把样品寄到这张名片上的地址吗？

　　毅冰：当然。我会通过邮件跟进并确认所有细节。感谢你们的光临！

　　客户 B：谢谢你，毅冰。我们会尽快联系你。

　　毅冰：期待与你们的合作！祝你们今天愉快！

Words & Phrases（词汇和句型）

take a look around 随意看看（展会期间最常用的表达之一）

a bit pricey 有点贵

long-term partnership 长期合作

down the road 未来、将来（口语化表达）

destination port 目的港（产品发货到客户指定的境外港口）

Chinglish Correction（中式英语纠错）

我相信我们能找到解决问题的办法。

【Chinglish】

I'm sure we can find a way to solve the problem.

【Native English】

I'm sure we can work something out.

▶ **毅冰补充：**

在跟客户沟通的过程中，需要避免的事情有两件。第一，逐字逐句直接翻译，有太多的翻译腔；第二，不够自然，没有把口语和书面语区分开来。

举个例子就很容易理解。假设你在便利店买饮料，随口就问一句，可乐多少钱？店员就会立刻回答你，3块5一罐。这就是很自然的口语。那如果用书面语呢？或许你就会说，"您好，我现在需要一罐可乐，用于饮用，能否请您告知我这一罐可乐的单价是多少？"

很显然，大家都会觉得，这太奇怪了，对吧？

这个句型，solve the problem，可以说，没有错，但是根据上下文语境来看，有的时候会显得不太自然，或者有那么一点沉重。解决问题的"解决"，口语中更多会用 fix，会用 improve，要根据上下文语境而定。而"问题"，也不一定是 problem，可以是 issue，也可以是 thing，甚至是其他。

work something out，某种程度上，就真的是想要"解决问题"。

9 碰上老客户，更需要拉近私人交情

故事背景

展会上，老客户 Jonathan 跟助理 Maggie 走了过来，毅冰连忙上前寒暄了几句。简单告知了目前进展中的订单和生产情况，也介绍了为了这次展会专门准备的新产品。与此同时，询问 Janathan 和 Maggie 这次的行程，约时间一起见个面，自然是必不可少的。

Dialogue:

Yibing: Hey Johnny, great to see you here!

Jonathan: Hi Yibing, nice to see you, too. Oh, this is Maggie, my assistant.

Yibing: Hi Maggie! We've been emailing back and forth for a while now!

Maggie: Yes, it's nice to finally meet you in person, Yibing!

Yibing: Likewise! Please, have a seat. Can I get you something to drink?

Jonathan: No, thanks. We're just going to take a quick look around first. But how about we meet tomorrow evening if you're free?

Yibing: Sure, that works. At your hotel?

Jonathan: Yes, we'll come back here in the afternoon to check out some of your new items, then we can have a meeting later. Oh, by the way, how's the running order for SP11075?

Yibing: Everything is on track. We should be able to deliver on time. I've already submitted the inspection booking and asked your forwarder to reserve the vessel.

Jonathan: Perfect.

Yibing: Also, I've got some newly designed outdoor products with color box packaging. Do you want me to bring those to the meeting at your hotel tomorrow? There are a few models we haven't displayed here as well.

Jonathan: Sounds good. I'll do a quick selection here first, and we'll go over everything tomorrow.

Yibing: Absolutely. By the way, how long will you be staying in China?

Jonathan: About a week. Then we're heading to Singapore to visit another supplier before flying back to the US. But for now, we've got to run.

Yibing: Got it. I'll see you tomorrow then!

参考译文 📖

毅冰： 嘿，Johnny，很高兴在这儿见到你！

Jonathan： 嗨，毅冰，很高兴见到你。噢，这是我的助理，Maggie。

毅冰： 你好，Maggie！我们之前一直在通过邮件联系呢！

Maggie： 是的，终于见到你了，毅冰！

毅冰： 同感！请坐。想喝点什么吗？

Jonathan： 不用了，谢谢。我们先随意看看。不过你明晚有时间吗？到时我们可以开个会。

毅冰： 当然可以。在你们酒店吗？

Jonathan： 对，明天下午我们会回来看看你们的新产品，然后晚上再开个会。对了，SP11075 这张订单进展怎么样了？

毅冰： 一切顺利。我们应该可以按时交货。我已经提交了验货申请，也通知了你们的指定货代安排订舱。

Jonathan： 完美。

毅冰： 另外，我们有一些新设计的户外产品，配有彩盒包装。明天开会时，需要我带过去吗？我们还有一些新款没有在这里展示。

Jonathan： 听起来不错。我先在这边快速选一下，明天我们再详细讨论。

毅冰： 没问题。对了，你们这次打算在中国待多久？

Jonathan： 大概一周。然后我们会去新加坡拜访另一个供应商，再回美国。不过现在我们得走了。

毅冰： 明白。那我们明天见！

Words & Phrases（词汇和句型）

Johnny 约翰尼（Jonathan 的昵称）

back and forth 来来回回地、往返地

in person 亲自、当面

Likewise! 我也有同感！（口语中十分常用，相当于"英雄所见略同"）

on track 按计划进行、进展顺利

Chinglish Correction（中式英语纠错）

我们清点一下人数。

【Chinglish】

Let's count the persons first.

【Native English】

Let's count the noses first.

▶ **毅冰补充：**

英语中有 count noses 的固定搭配，指"点人数""点名"。假设跟客户在酒店大堂碰面，准备搭车出发去工厂，为了确保所有人都在，没有遗漏，或许要跟客户说，你要先清点一下人数，看看有没有到齐。这样的场景下，这句地道的口语就可以轻而易举用上了。

10 给客户看样品，不能靠苍白的自我陈述

故事背景

展会上，一个客户走进展位，询问了货架上一款太阳能灯的价格，也了解了相关的参数和最小起订量，让毅冰拿样品给他看。随后客户提出修改包装的要求，跟毅冰做了进一步的讨论。

Dialogue:

Yibing: Hi there! How can I assist you today?

Stephy: Hi, here's my business card.

Yibing: Thank you! Here's mine. So, what can I help you with today? Are you looking for something specific?

Stephy: Yes, I'm interested in your solar lights, especially for outdoor use. I noticed this model, can you tell me more about it?

Yibing: Absolutely. This is one of our best-selling models for outdoor applications. It's equipped with high-efficiency solar panels and a durable, weather-resistant design. It's quite popular in both Europe and the US markets. We've enhanced the light output while maintaining a sleek, compact form factor.

Stephy: Interesting. What's the price per unit?

Yibing: The price for this model is $12.50 per unit, FOB Shanghai, with a minimum order quantity of 3000 pieces. That includes standard packaging—one piece per color box.

Stephy: I see. How flexible are you on the MOQ? We're considering a smaller initial run to test the market, perhaps 1500 units. Would you be open to that?

Yibing: For first-time orders, we can consider reducing the MOQ to 2000 units. However, for anything lower than that, the cost per unit might increase slightly due to production setup fees.

Stephy: Hmm, I understand. Could you share the price adjustment for 1500 units? I need to evaluate the overall cost-effectiveness before committing.

Yibing: Certainly. For 1500 units, the price would increase to $12.70 per unit, due to higher packaging and production overhead on smaller batches. If that works for you, we can proceed with those terms.

Stephy: That's a bit higher than I expected, especially when factoring in shipping and duties. Is there any room to negotiate if we increase the volume later? Say, if we reorder 5000 units within six months?

Yibing: Sure. We're happy to discuss price adjustments for future bulk orders. If your reorder exceeds 5000 units, we could offer a discount, likely bringing the unit price down to $12.30. We're always keen to build long-term partnerships.

Stephy: That sounds more reasonable. I also noticed that you pack one piece per box. Could we explore alternative packaging options? We're considering selling this as a two-pack, so a larger box would be needed.

Yibing: We can definitely accommodate that. Packing two units in one larger color box would reduce packaging costs per unit. I'll need to confirm the exact cost with our supplier, but typically the savings are noticeable. Do you have any specific requirements for the box dimensions or design?

Stephy: Yes, we'd like to keep the packaging simple but sturdy, with a focus on eco-friendly materials. Can you also make sure the packaging aligns with EU regulations for recyclability?

Yibing: Of course, we've worked with various clients in Europe, so we're familiar with the packaging requirements there. We use recycled materials for our color boxes, and they meet all EU sustainability standards. I'll check with our packaging supplier and send you the revised pricing and options by email.

Stephy: Perfect. Lastly, what's the lead time for production and shipping to the UK?

Yibing: Once we confirm the order and finalize the packaging details, production will take about 30-35 days. Shipping to the UK via sea freight usually takes 25-30 days. If you're in a rush, we could explore air freight options, though that would significantly increase your shipping costs.

Stephy: I'll stick with sea freight for now. I'll need a detailed quote with these updates before making a decision. When can I expect it?

Yibing: I'll have everything prepared and emailed to you within two business days. We'll include pricing for both 1500 and 3000 units, packaging options, and the lead times.

Stephy: Great, thanks. I'll review everything and get back to you soon. Let's see if we can make this work.

Yibing: Sounds good. I'm looking forward to working with you. Feel free to reach out if you have any further questions.

参考译文 📖

毅冰：你好！有什么我可以帮忙的吗？

Stephy：你好，这是我的名片。

毅冰：谢谢！也请收一下我的名片。那么，今天有什么可以为你效劳的吗？你是在寻找什么特定的产品吗？

Stephy：是的，我对你们的太阳能灯感兴趣，特别是户外使用的那种。我注意到这个款式，你能详细介绍一下吗？

毅冰：当然可以。这款是我们最畅销的户外应用产品之一。它配备了高效的太阳能电池板，设计坚固耐用，防风雨。在欧洲和美国市场很受欢迎。我们提升了光输出，同时保持了时尚、紧凑的外观设计。

Stephy：听起来不错。价格是多少？

毅冰：这款的价格是每件 12.50 美元，FOB 上海，最小起订量是 3000 件。标准包装是一件一个彩盒。

Stephy：我明白了。最小起订量方面，你们能灵活处理吗？我们考虑先批量试单，大约 1500 件。你们能接受吗？

毅冰：对于首次订单，我们可以考虑把最小起订量降到 2000 件。不过，如果低于这个数量，单价可能会略有上升，因为生产设置成本较高。

Stephy：嗯，我理解。你能告诉我 1500 件的价格调整吗？我需要评估整体的成本效益才能决定。

毅冰：当然。1500 件的价格将上调至每件 12.70 美元，因为小批量的包装和生产费用较高。如果你觉得可以接受，我们可以按照这些条款继续。

Stephy：这个价格比我预想的要高一些，特别是考虑到运输和关税。如果我们之后加大订单量，比如在六个月内再订购 5000 件，是否有商量的余地？

毅冰：当然，我们很乐意为未来的大批量订单讨论价格调整。如果你再次订购超过 5000 件，我们可以提供折扣，单价可能会降到每件 12.30 美元。我们非常愿意建立长期的合作关系。

Stephy：这样听起来更合理一些。我还注意到你们的标准包装是一件一个彩盒。我们考虑把它做成双件装，所以可能需要一个更大的彩盒。你们能做到吗？

毅冰：当然可以。我们可以按你的要求提供双件包装。包装成本会有所降低，我需要和我们的供应商确认具体费用，但节省费用是肯定的。你对包装尺寸或设计有特别要求吗？

Stephy：有的，我们希望包装简单但坚固，重点要使用环保材料。你们的包装能符合欧盟的可持续标准吗？

毅冰：没问题，我们和欧洲的客户有合作，熟悉那边的包装要求。我们使用的是再生材料，符合欧盟的可持续标准。我会和我们的包装供应商确认，之后通过邮件把价格和选项发给你。

Stephy：很好。最后问一下，生产和运输到英国的时间是多久？

毅冰：一旦确认订单并确定包装细节，生产时间为 30 到 35 天。海运到英国通常需要 25 到 30 天。如果你赶时间，我们也可以考虑选择空运，但那样会大幅增加运输成本。

Stephy：目前我还是会选择海运。我需要一份详细的报价，包括这些更新的信息，才能做决定。什么时候能发给我？

毅冰：我会在两个工作日内把所有内容准备好并发到你的邮箱。我们会把 1500 件和 3000 件的报价、包装选项以及交货时间都包含在内。

Stephy：太好了，谢谢。我会审核所有内容，并尽快回复你。希望我们可以达成合作。

毅冰：没问题。期待与你合作。如果你有其他问题，随时联系我。

Words & Phrases（词汇和句型）

business card 名片

first-time orders 初次订单

increase the volume 增加（产品）数量

eco-friendly materials 环保材料

sea freight 海运

Chinglish Correction（中式英语纠错）

请跟进一下，看看测试结果如何。

【Chinglish】

Please follow this case, and see the result of testing.

【Native English】

Please chase this up and get the testing result.

▶ **毅冰补充：**

英语口语中，chase up 是一个固定短语，可以表示跟进某件事。比如寄了样品给客户，提供了快递单号，让客户跟进一下，就可以用 Please chase it up. 这个地道的表达。

11　介绍参展产品，靠大声吆喝是不够的

故事背景 🖉

毅冰在展位上站了一整天，接待了几十波来来往往的客户，已经累得喉咙冒烟。刚拿了瓶水喝了一口，又有客户走了进来。毅冰连忙放下迎上前，继续卖力工作，给客户介绍产品。

Dialogue:

Yibing: Good afternoon, sir. Welcome to our booth! How can I help you today?

Henry: Hi there, I'm looking for some new solar lights, preferably in the 5 to 8 US dollar range. Do you have anything that <u>fits the bill</u>?

Yibing: Absolutely, we've got a wide selection in that <u>price range</u>. Just to get a better idea of your needs, what type of packaging do you usually go for? We offer both color boxes and double blister packs, depending on the market.

Henry: Well, for our European customers, they tend to lean toward color boxes—it has more retail appeal there. But for the US market, double blister packaging works better, especially for <u>big box retailers</u>.

Yibing: Makes sense. Let me pull out a few options for you. This one here is a big hit in the US, and these two are doing really well across Europe. All of them fall within your price range, and they're packaged exactly as you've described. What do you think?

Henry: These look solid. Who are you supplying to in the US, if you don't mind me asking?

Yibing: No problem. We're currently working with Target, Kmart, and a couple of major importers. These models are actually some of their best-sellers, especially during peak seasons like spring and summer.

Henry: That's good to know. I like the sound of that. I'll need to run some numbers, but it sounds promising so far. Could you send me a detailed offer sheet soon?

Yibing: Absolutely, I'll have that sent over by tomorrow. Here's my card, and if you could give me yours, I'll make sure all the details are spot on.

Henry: Sure, here you go. Also, in terms of lead time, what are we looking at? I need to make sure we can hit some tight delivery windows for the holiday promotions.

Yibing: Our standard production lead time is around 30 to 35 days, but if you're in a rush, we can prioritize your order. Just give me the specifics on when you need the goods, and I'll check with our factory to see if we can expedite it. We've done that for some of our larger clients before.

Henry: Great, I'll confirm the dates with my team and let you know. Another quick question—are you able to offer any kind of discount for bulk orders? If we like these samples, we're looking at placing a larger order in the next quarter.

Yibing: Definitely, we can be flexible on pricing if you're placing a high-volume order. Once we get to quantities over 10000 pieces, we can work out a discount structure. I'll include some preliminary pricing tiers in the offer sheet, so you have a clear picture.

Henry: Perfect, that's what I needed to hear. I'll look for your email and let's see if we can move forward on this.

Yibing: Sounds like a plan. I'll get everything over to you ASAP. If you need anything else, feel free to reach out—happy to help in any way I can.

Henry: Thanks, Yibing. I'll be in touch once I've reviewed everything.

Yibing: My pleasure, Henry. I look forward to working with you!

参考译文 📖

毅冰： 下午好，先生。欢迎光临我们的展位！有什么可以帮你的吗?

Henry： 你好，我想找一些新款的太阳能灯，价格在 5 到 8 美元之间。你们有符合这个价位的产品吗?

毅冰： 当然有，我们有很多款式都在这个价格范围内。为了更好地了解你的需求，你通常选择哪种包装方式? 我们有彩盒和双泡壳包装，具体取决于市场需求。

Henry： 嗯，对于我们的欧洲客户，他们更倾向于彩盒包装——在零售店里看起来更有吸引力。但对于美国市场，双泡壳包装效果更好，尤其是对于大型零售商。

毅冰： 明白了。我给你推荐几款产品。这款产品在美国市场非常受欢迎，而这两款产品在欧洲市场也卖得很好。它们都在你的预算范围内，包装方式也完全符合你的需求。你觉得怎么样?

Henry： 这些看起来不错。冒昧问一下，你们在美国都供应给哪些客户?

毅冰： 没问题。目前我们与 Target、Kmart，以及几家大型进口商都有合作。这些款式其实是他们在春夏旺季的热销产品。

Henry： 这很好。听起来不错。我需要计算一下成本，但目前看起来很有前景。你能尽快给我发一份详细的报价单吗?

毅冰： 当然，我明天就发你。这是我的名片，如果能给我你的名片，我会确保所有细节都准确无误。

Henry： 好的，这是我的名片。另外，关于交货时间，大概需要多久? 我得确保能赶上节假日促销的紧急发货期。

毅冰： 我们标准的生产周期是 30 到 35 天，但如果你着急，我们可以优先处理你的订单。只要你告诉我具体的要货时间，我会与工厂确认是否能够加急处理。我们之前也为一些大客户加过急。

Henry：太好了，我确认日期后告诉你。另外，我还有个问题——如果是大批量订单，能否提供一些折扣？如果这些样品合适的话，我们打算在下个季度加大订量。

毅冰：当然，如果你下的是大批量订单，我们在价格上可以灵活一些。当订单量超过 10000 件时，我们可以商讨一个折扣方案。我会在报价单中附上一些初步的价格分级，这样你会有一个清晰的了解。

Henry：完美，这正是我想听的。我先等你的邮件，然后我们再看看接下来如何推进。

毅冰：听起来不错。我会尽快把所有资料发给你。如果还有其他需要，随时联系我——我很乐意提供帮助。

Henry：谢谢你，毅冰。等我看完资料后再联系你。

毅冰：不客气，Henry。期待与你合作！

Words & Phrases（词汇和句型）

fits the bill 表示"符合要求"（非常口语化的表达）

price range 价格区间

big box retailers 大型零售商

detailed offer sheet 详细的报价单（也可以说 offer sheet in detail）

high-volume order 大订单

Chinglish Correction（中式英语纠错）

我们马上到你公司了。

【Chinglish】

We will come to your company soon.

【Native English】

We are coming to your company soon.

▶ **毅冰补充：**

英语中，come 和 go 这两个动词比较特殊，可以用现在进行时表示将来。一般句子里出现 come 或者 go，是很少用 will 加动词原形的，可以理解为习惯问题。

12 忙不过来的时候，要引导和介绍同事跟进

故事背景

展会进行得如火如荼。又是一天上午，某个客户走进展位，向毅冰询问野营灯的价格。由于毅冰在公司负责太阳能灯的业务，并不擅长野营灯，于是就介绍了同事 Athena 给客户，让他们直接沟通。接下来，Athena 就顺理成章，跟客户讨论了野营灯的一些相关情况。

Dialogue:

Yibing: Good morning! How can I assist you today?

Jack: Morning. I'm Jack, and here's my business card. I'm interested in the price for these two <u>camping lamps</u>.

Yibing: Nice to meet you, Jack. These particular items are handled by my colleague. Let me introduce you to her.

Jack: Sure, that works.

Yibing: Athena, can you join us for a moment? Jack is looking for the pricing details on these two camping lamps. Here's his card; please provide him with the product overview.

Jack: Hi, Athena. Nice to meet you!

Athena: Hi Jack, great to see you here. Let me walk you through the details. These two lamps are designed specifically for <u>portability</u>— they come with built-in handles and car adaptors, making them ideal for camping or outdoor use. The larger model is priced at $12 per unit, and the smaller one is $9.

Jack: Does that price include the entire set?

Athena: Yes, the price covers one lamp, one <u>power adaptor</u>, and one <u>car plug</u> in each package.

Jack: Got it. How many units of the smaller model fit into a 20-foot container?

Athena: Let me check... For the small model, you can fit approximately 1500 pieces in a 20-foot container.

Jack: So, for a 40-foot container, that would double to around 3000 pieces, right?

Athena: Exactly, that's correct.

Jack: Great. Please send me a detailed offer sheet including pricing, specifications, and lead times. Also, I'd like to request two samples of the smaller lamp for testing. By the way, have these products passed UL or ETL certification?

Athena: Yes, the plugs have ETL certification, which ensures they meet North American safety standards.

Jack: Perfect. I'll need that documentation as well for my internal review. What's your usual lead time for production?

Athena: Typically, our production lead time is 35 to 40 days, depending on the order volume. For large orders like this, we can discuss scheduling to prioritize your shipment if necessary.

Jack: That sounds good. I'll review the offer sheet once I receive it, and we can take it from there. Thanks, Athena.

Athena: You're very welcome, Jack. I'll follow up with the detailed information and samples shortly. Feel free to reach out if you have any further questions <u>in the meantime</u>.

参考译文 📖

毅冰： 早上好，有什么是我可以帮忙的吗？

Jack： 早上好。我是 Jack，这是我的名片。我对这两款露营灯的价格感兴趣。

毅冰： 很高兴认识您，Jack。这些产品是由我的同事负责的。让我来为你介绍一下她吧。

Jack： 好的，没问题。

毅冰： Athena，能过来一下吗？Jack 想了解这两款露营灯的价格细节。这是他的名片，请为他介绍一下产品。

Jack： 你好，Athena。很高兴见到你！

Athena： 你好，Jack，很高兴在这里见到你。让我为你介绍一下这两款产品。它们为便携式设计，带有手柄和车载适配器，非常适合露营或在户外使用。大号款每个售价 12 美元，小号款是 9 美元。

Jack： 这个价格是包含整套配件吗？

Athena： 是的，报价包括一盏灯、一个电源适配器和一个车载插头，所有配件都在包装内。

Jack： 明白了。那么，小号款的数量在一个 20 尺的集装箱里能装多少件？

Athena： 让我查一下……小号款在一个 20 尺的集装箱大概可以装 1500 件。

Jack： 那么，40 尺的集装箱大约是 3000 件，对吧？

Athena： 是的，没错。

Jack： 好的。请发送一份详细的报价单给我，包括价格、规格和交货时间。另外，我还想要两个小号灯的样品用于测试。对了，这些产品通过 UL 或 ETL 认证了吗？

Athena： 是的，插头已经通过 ETL 认证，符合北美的安全标准。

Jack：很好。我还需要这些认证的文件，用于我们内部审核。你们的生产周期通常是多久？

Athena：通常我们的生产周期是 35 到 40 天，具体取决于订单量。像您这样的大订单，如果需要，我们可以讨论优先安排货期。

Jack：听起来不错。我收到报价单后会进行审核评估，然后我们再继续讨论。谢谢你，Athena。

Athena：不客气，Jack。我会尽快跟进详细信息和样品。与此同时，如果你有其他问题，随时联系我。

Words & Phrases（词汇和句型）

camping lamp 野营灯、露营灯

portability 便携性

power adaptor 电源适配器

car plug 车载充电器

in the meantime 与此同时

Chinglish Correction（中式英语纠错）

你能算一下这个订单的总立方数吗？

【Chinglish】

Could you calculate the CBM for this order?

【Native English】

Could you work out the CBM for this order?

▶ **毅冰补充：**

计算体积，calculate 这个词可以用，语法没错，大家可以听懂，但是并非最佳选项。而 work out 这个短语，用来表示"计算""测算""解决""算出"等，反而是英语母语人士在电邮和口语里经常使用的。

展会上直接报价，你真的够专业吗

故事背景

参展期间，刚接待完一波客户，又有一位新客户走进展位。不同的是，客户带了自己的样品，请毅冰报价。毅冰详细核算完成本，报了一个大致的价格，其他相关细节还需要回去跟技术人员和采购部同事确认后。这样才能有更准确的报价。

Dialogue:

Yibing: Good morning!

Nick: Morning. So, you're in the lighting business, right?

Yibing: Yep, that's us.

Nick: Are you a factory or more of a trading company?

Yibing: Actually, we're <u>a bit of both</u>. We manufacture and also handle trading, plus we've got our own R&D team <u>in-house</u>.

Nick: That's good to know. How many people are you running with?

Yibing: We've got about 250 employees, including our office and factory staff.

Nick: Nice. So, can you help me check the pricing on these two lamps?

Yibing: Sure! I have to say, the glass design on these is really sharp.

Nick: Thanks, we're pretty happy with it. We're looking at around 50000 units. Can you give me your best price for that quantity?

Yibing: Wow, that's a solid order. Please, take a seat, want some water or coffee while I check?

Nick: Water would be great, thanks.

Yibing: <u>Sure thing</u>. Alright, so the body diameter is 17cm, tube diameter is 2cm, and the thickness is 1mm. What are you thinking for the LED? Any specific requirements?

Nick: We want to keep it the same as this one—1 watt.

Yibing: Got it. Now, just to clarify—do you have a preference on the LED source? We can do Chinese-made, US-made, or even German-made. The pricing varies depending on the origin.

Nick: Let's stick with something competitive. Give me the best option you've got without <u>breaking the bank</u>.

Yibing: Will do. And for the packaging—do you want one piece per three-layer color box, with 24 pieces in an outer carton? That's our <u>usual setup</u>.

Nick: Actually, could you add an inner box? I'm thinking 12 pieces per inner box, then 24 per outer carton. It'll keep things more secure during shipping.

Yibing: No problem, I'll make a note of that. So, based on the specs you've given me, the rough estimate is around $3.90 per unit. I'll need to run this by our engineering and purchasing teams to get a more accurate breakdown for you.

Nick: Sounds good. Just let me know once you've got the final numbers.

Yibing: Sure thing. By the way, any chance you can leave the sample with us for reference?

Nick: Unfortunately, I only have the one with me. But I'll send a sample directly to your factory as soon as I get back to the office.

Yibing: Perfect. Thanks for that, Nick. I'll have the finalized offer over to you shortly.

Nick: Great, I'll keep an eye out for it. Thanks, Yibing.

Yibing: Anytime, Nick. Looking forward to working with you.

参考译文 📖

毅冰： 早上好!

Nick： 早上好。你们是做照明产品的，对吧?

毅冰： 是的，没错。

Nick： 你们是工厂还是贸易公司?

毅冰： 实际上，我们是两者兼具。我们有自己的工厂，也负责贸易开发，还拥有自己的研发团队。

Nick： 很好，了解了。你们有多少员工?

毅冰： 我们大概有 250 名员工，包括办公室和工厂的人员。

Nick： 不错。能帮我查一下这两款灯的价格吗?

毅冰： 当然! 顺便说一句，这个灯的玻璃的设计很漂亮。

Nick： 谢谢，我们对这个设计也很满意。我们的预期数量是 50000 件。基于这个数量，能给我一个最优的价格吗?

毅冰： 哇，这订单量不错。请先坐一下。我帮你查一查，想喝点什么? 水还是咖啡?

Nick： 水就好，谢谢。

毅冰： 好的，马上给你。这个灯的主体直径是 17 厘米，管子的直径是 2 厘米，壁厚是 1 毫米。关于 LED 灯，你有什么具体要求吗?

Nick： 我们想跟这款保持一样——1 瓦的功率。

毅冰： 明白。不过，我想确认一下，你对 LED 灯的产地有要求吗? 我们可以用中国、美国或德国生产的。价格会因产地不同而有差异。

Nick： 选一个性价比高的吧。别太贵。

毅冰： 没问题。至于包装，你要每个装一个三层彩盒，外箱里装 24 个吗? 这是我们常规的包装方式。

Nick： 其实，能不能加一个内盒? 我想每 12 个装一个内盒，然后再 24 个装一个外箱。这样运输时会更稳妥。

毅冰：没问题，我会记下来。根据目前的规格，预估单价大概是 3.90 美元。不过我还需要跟我们的工程师和采购团队确认每个部分的成本，之后会给你一个更精确的报价。

Nick：听起来不错。等你拿到最终价格再告诉我。

毅冰：没问题。顺便问一下，你能把样品留给我们参考吗？

Nick：不好意思，我现在手上只有这一件。但我一回到办公室，就把样品寄到你们工厂。

毅冰：完美。谢谢你，Nick。我会尽快把最终的报价发给你。

Nick：很好，我会留意的。谢谢你，毅冰。

毅冰：不客气，Nick。期待与你合作。

Words & Phrases（词汇和句型）

a bit of both 两者兼具、两者兼备

in-house 内部的、内部存在的

sure thing 没问题（口语中常见）

break the bank 指"价格非常昂贵"

usual setup 常规设置（根据上下文，这里指"常规的包装"）

Chinglish Correction（中式英语纠错）

现在很晚了，您应该在家休息了。

【Chinglish】

It is very late now, and you have to have a rest at home.

【Native English】

It is very late, you should be at home relaxing by now.

毅冰补充：

have a rest 是人们喜欢用的英语短语，每次提到"休息"，第一个想到的

就是 have a rest。

在英语中，have a rest 只是表达"小憩""稍微休息一会"。文中这句话的目的是告诉对方，现在太晚了，应该好好休息了，我不再打扰你了。这表示的是一个相对长的时间段，就需要用 relax 的动名词形式，表示"放松""休息"。

14 | 预约见面时间，把握每一次开发机会

故事背景

展会最后一天，来过毅冰展位的一个德国客户 Christina 再次过来，跟毅冰预约时间，打算拜访毅冰的公司，并参观样品间。毅冰欣然接受，现场简单沟通了时间和后续大致的行程安排。

Dialogue:

Yibing: Hi Christina, glad to see you again!

Christina: Hey Yibing, I wanted to check with you about my upcoming business trip. I'll be visiting suppliers in Shanghai and Zhejiang for about seven days. Is it possible to stop by your company while I'm there?

Yibing: Absolutely! We'd love to have you. You can tour our factory and check out some of our latest items in the showroom. I'm sure you'll find it interesting.

Christina: That sounds perfect! I'm flying to Shanghai next Monday, and I've got meetings with two suppliers then. I think next Wednesday works for me to visit your place.

Yibing: Great, we can arrange a pick-up for you that day. By the way, where are you staying in Shanghai? Do you need any help with booking a hotel?

Christina: No need, thanks. I've already booked a Deluxe Room at EDITION. Do you know the hotel?

Yibing: Oh yes, it's a fantastic choice! Very upscale.

Christina: Is it downtown?

Yibing: Yes, it's in the Bund area, right in the heart of Shanghai.

Christina: How far is it from your office?

Yibing: It's about a one-hour drive, depending on traffic.

Christina: Got it. I'll give you a call tonight to confirm the exact time.

Yibing: Sounds good. Looking forward to seeing you!

参考译文 📖

毅冰：你好，Christina，很高兴再次见到你！

Christina：嗨，毅冰，我想和你确认一下我的商务行程。我将去上海和浙江拜访供应商，大概会待七天。我可以顺便参观你们公司吗？

毅冰：当然可以！欢迎你来参观。你可以参观我们的工厂，还可以在我们的展厅里看看最新的产品。我相信你会感兴趣的。

Christina：听起来很棒！我下周一会飞上海，去见两个供应商。估计下周三有时间去你们公司。

毅冰：太好了，我们可以安排那天来接你。对了，你在上海住在哪里？需要我们帮你预订酒店吗？

Christina：不用了，谢谢。我已经预订了上海艾迪逊酒店的豪华房。你知道这家酒店吗？

毅冰：当然知道，很棒的选择！非常高档的酒店。

Christina：是在市中心吗？

毅冰：是的，就在上海外滩附近，市中心的位置。

Christina：离你们公司有多远？

毅冰：开车大概一个小时，具体看交通情况。

Christina：好的。我今晚打电话给你，确认具体时间。

毅冰：没问题。期待见到你！

Words & Phrases（词汇和句型）

upcoming business trip 即将来临的商务行程

stop by 拜访、走访（是一种非正式的表达）

latest items 最新的产品

arrange a pick-up 安排接送

downtown 市中心

Chinglish Correction（中式英语纠错）

我来买单吧！

【Chinglish】

I will pay for it!

【Native English】

It's my treat!

▶ **毅冰补充：**

买单这个词，的确是 pay for the bill，但是口语中很少这么说，而是有四个类似的表达，可以灵活使用。

1) It's my treat!

2) It's my turn!

3) I will spring for it!

4) It's on me!

这四句的含义接近，都可以在口语场景里灵活使用。

客户工厂拜访，
现场交流的绝佳
策略

15 确认接机事宜，打造成功的第一印象

故事背景

德国客户 Nicole 计划来毅冰公司拜访，一周前已跟毅冰约好时间，并安排好相关的行程。Nicole 的航班是从法兰克福飞香港，中转停留后第二天飞上海。Nicole 到香港的当晚就接到毅冰的电话，确认最终的行程并约定接机事宜。

Dialogue:

Yibing: Hey Nicole, it's Yibing. Have you made it to Hong Kong?

Nicole: Hi Yibing. Yeah, I just got to the hotel. I'm about to <u>take a shower</u> and <u>grab a bite</u> to eat—feeling pretty <u>wiped out</u>.

Yibing: I can imagine! How's the trip been so far?

Nicole: Honestly? It was exhausting. More than 11 hours from Frankfurt to Hong Kong, and then the traffic from the airport to the hotel was insane. I didn't expect it to take so long!

Yibing: Yeah, the traffic in Hong Kong can be rough, especially at peak times. But hey, you're almost there—just one more flight and you'll be in Shanghai. Once you're here, everything will be smooth sailing.

How's the hotel, by the way?

Nicole: It's nice! A bit smaller than I expected, but comfortable. I'm just happy to be off the plane and lying in a real bed. I think a good meal and a long sleep will fix me up.

Yibing: That sounds perfect. I bet you'll feel much better after some rest. I just wanted to re-confirm your flight details and make sure everything's set for tomorrow. You're arriving on Cathay Pacific flight CX316 at 11:05 a.m., right?

Nicole: Yep, that's correct!

Yibing: Awesome. We'll have someone from the team meet you at Pudong Airport and handle the pick-up. Is there anything else you need me to arrange for tomorrow?

Nicole: No, I think I'm all set for now. Just looking forward to getting to Shanghai and kicking off the meetings.

Yibing: Great! Once you get here, we'll have everything ready for you. The hotel is all arranged, and we've scheduled meetings with the suppliers. You'll have some time to relax before diving into work.

Nicole: Perfect, that sounds good. I'm really looking forward to meeting everyone in person and seeing the factory. By the way, do you know what the weather's like in Shanghai right now?

Yibing: It's been pretty mild, around 18°C, so not too hot or cold. You'll probably just need a light jacket, but I'll double-check the forecast for tomorrow and let you know if there's any change.

Nicole: That's helpful, thanks. I'll make sure to pack accordingly.

Yibing: No problem. Just focus on resting tonight—you've got a big day ahead. We're all excited to have you here!

Nicole: Thanks, Yibing. I'll catch up with you tomorrow. And hey, make sure you get some rest too!

Yibing: Will do! Safe travels and see you in Shanghai tomorrow.

参考译文 📖

毅冰：嗨，Nicole，我是毅冰。你到香港了吗？

Nicole：嗨，毅冰。是的，我刚到酒店。正准备去洗个澡然后找点东西吃——感觉整个人都累坏了。

毅冰：我能想象！一路过来怎么样？

Nicole：说实话？真的很累。从法兰克福到香港飞了 11 个多小时，然后从机场到酒店的交通也很糟糕。没想到会花这么长时间！

毅冰：是啊，香港的交通特别在高峰的时候确实很堵。不过，别担心，你马上就到上海，再飞一程就好了。等到了这边，一切都会顺利的。对了，酒店怎么样？

Nicole：挺不错的！房间比我想象的要小一点，但很舒服。我现在只想躺在床上，好好休息一下。我觉得吃顿美食再好好睡一觉，应该就恢复过来了。

毅冰：听起来不错。我敢打赌，睡一觉之后你就会感觉好多了。我只是想重新确认一下你的航班信息，确保明天一切都安排好了。你是乘坐国泰航空 CX316 航班，上午 11:05 到，对吧？

Nicole：是的，没错！

毅冰：太好了。我们会安排团队的人在浦东机场接你并负责接送。明天你还有什么需要我们安排的吗？

Nicole：不用，我现在一切都准备好了。就等到上海后开始开会。

毅冰：太好了！你到了之后，我们会为你准备好一切。酒店已经安排好了，我们也安排了和供应商的会议。你可以先放松一下，然后再开始工作。

Nicole：完美，听起来很棒。我很期待见到大家，也想参观一下工厂。对了，你知道上海现在的天气怎么样吗？

毅冰：最近天气比较暖和，大概 18 摄氏度，不冷也不热。你可能只需要带一件薄外套，但我会再查一下明天的天气预报，如果有变化的话会告诉你。

Nicole：这很有帮助，谢谢。我会根据天气准备好行李。

毅冰：不客气。你今晚就好好休息吧——明天是大日子。我们都很期待你来！

Nicole：谢谢你，毅冰。明天见。对了，你也要好好休息！

毅冰：没问题！祝你旅途愉快，明天上海见！

Words & Phrases（词汇和句型）

take a shower 洗澡、淋浴

grab a bite 吃点东西（通常指快速吃一些简单的东西，很地道的口语表达）

wiped out 筋疲力尽（相当于 exhausted）

Cathay Pacific 国泰航空

kick off the meetings 开始开会（kick off 原意是足球场上的"中场开球"，在商务英语中引申为"开工""开动""复工"等）

Chinglish Correction（中式英语纠错）

因为时差没倒过来，我现在好困。

【Chinglish】

Because of the time problem, I feel so tired.

【Native English】

I'm really tired because of the jet lag.

▶ **毅冰补充：**

英语中，时差有一个专门的单词 jet lag，也可以拼成 jet-lag。克服时差，是 get over jet-lag。

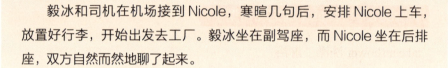

故事背景 ✎

> 毅冰和司机在机场接到 Nicole，寒暄几句后，安排 Nicole 上车，放置好行李，开始出发去工厂。毅冰坐在副驾座，而 Nicole 坐在后排座，双方自然而然地聊了起来。

Dialogue:

Yibing: How was your trip? Everything go smoothly?

Nicole: Yeah, it was great. I actually enjoyed it. The food on the plane was <u>surprisingly good</u>.

Yibing: That's nice! I always think an extra night in Hong Kong helps with the jet lag. And of course, you can never go wrong with some <u>authentic Cantonese food</u>.

Nicole: Definitely, but I've got to say, the hotel prices in Hong Kong are <u>through the roof</u>. I mean, it's beautiful here, but wow, expensive.

Yibing: Oh, where did you stay?

Nicole: I stayed at <u>The Upper House</u>. Have you heard of it?

Yibing: Wow, The Upper House? That's one of the most luxurious hotels in <u>Admiralty</u>. Must've been quite an experience! How was it?

Nicole: It was amazing, really. The service was top-notch, and the view from my room was just breathtaking. But for the price? Yeah, I can see why people say it's one of the most expensive hotels in Hong Kong.

Yibing: I can imagine! Well, at least you got the full Hong Kong experience.

Nicole: Oh, for sure. It's just that staying there kind of made me think twice about ordering room service—didn't want to add more to the bill!

Yibing: (laughing...) I totally get it. So, what's the plan for now? Want us to drive you to the hotel so you can check in, relax, and freshen up?

Nicole: Actually, I'd rather head straight to the factory first. I feel like getting the work part done before I settle in.

Yibing: That's probably a good idea. Once the factory tour's done, you can fully relax at the hotel without any unfinished business hanging over your head.

Nicole: Exactly. I'd rather focus on work first, then I can unwind later.

Yibing: Makes sense. The factory's about an hour's drive from here, as long as traffic isn't too crazy. Do you want to grab something to eat on the way, or should we go straight there?

Nicole: Let's head straight to the factory. I had a quick bite at the airport, so I'm good for now. But thanks for asking!

Yibing: Perfect. And after the factory tour, we'll have everything arranged for you to head to the hotel and rest. If you need anything else, just let me know, and we'll take care of it.

Nicole: Appreciate it, Yibing. I'm looking forward to seeing the factory and the team. It's always better to see things in person, you know?

Yibing: Absolutely. We're really excited to have you here. It's a great opportunity to show you what we've been working on and how we can support your plans moving forward.

Nicole: Great, can't wait to see it all. Let's get this day started!

参考译文 📖

毅冰: 旅途怎么样？一切顺利吧？

Nicole: 是的，非常好。我居然还挺享受的。飞机上的食物出乎意料

地好吃。

毅冰：那真不错！我一直觉得在香港多住一晚对倒时差很有帮助。而且，你还能吃到正宗的粤菜，简直不能更好了。

Nicole：当然，不过香港的酒店真的贵得离谱。这里确实很美，但价格实在太高了。

毅冰：哦，你住哪儿了？

Nicole：我住在奕居。你听说过吗？

毅冰：哇，奕居？那可是金钟最豪华的酒店之一啊！一定是一次很棒的体验吧？感觉怎么样？

Nicole：真的很棒。服务一流，而且我房间的景色美得惊人。不过话说回来，价格确实也很高，难怪大家都说这是香港最贵的酒店之一。

毅冰：我能想象！不过至少你完全体验到了香港的豪华。

Nicole：是啊，没错。就是住在那里，让我都不敢再点客房服务——不想再多加账单了！

毅冰：（笑）我完全理解。所以现在你打算怎么安排？要不要我们先送你去酒店，办理入住、放下行李，然后洗个澡放松一下？

Nicole：其实，我更想先去工厂看看。我觉得要先把工作搞定一部分，再去放松。

毅冰：这确实是个好主意。等工厂参观结束后，你就可以完全放松，不用再考虑工作上的事情了。

Nicole：完全同意。我想先专注于工作，然后再好好休息。

毅冰：有道理。工厂离这里大概开车一个小时，前提是路况不差。你要不要路上先吃点东西，还是我们直接去工厂？

Nicole：我们直接去工厂吧。我在机场简单吃了一点儿，现在还不饿。谢谢你的关心！

毅冰：好的，没问题。参观完工厂之后，我们会安排送你回酒店休息。如果有其他需要，随时告诉我，我们会安排好。

Nicole：谢谢你，毅冰。我很期待参观工厂和见到团队的成员。亲自去看总比在网上了解好得多，你懂的。

毅冰：完全同意。我们也非常期待你能来。这是一个展示我们近期工作的好机会，也能让你看看我们如何支持你未来的计划。

Nicole：太好了，我等不及要去看看了。我们开始今天的行程吧！

Words & Phrases（词汇和句型）

surprisingly good 出乎意料地好

authentic Cantonese food 地道的粤菜

through the roof 直线上升（这里表示价格非常高）

The Upper House 奕居（香港知名酒店之一）

Admiralty 金钟（香港核心区域，西边是中环，东边是湾仔）

Chinglish Correction（中式英语纠错）

Nicole 对毅冰安排的接机大加赞赏。

【Chinglish】

Nicole admired Yibing for the pick-up in the airport.

【Native English】

Nicole cried up Yibing for the pick-up in the airport.

▶ **毅冰补充：**

口语中，cry up 是一个固定搭配，表示"大力表扬""大加赞赏"。而 admire 作为动词虽有"称赞""赞美"的意思，但在表现力上还是略有欠缺。

一些常用的短语，要牢记并灵活使用。

17 到访工厂，学习初次寒暄的技巧

故事背景

> 毅冰跟 Nicole 到工厂后，司机停好车，就请两人下车。这时候，工厂的同事们都已经在楼下等候。毅冰带着 Nicole 上前，简单介绍同事们给 Nicole 认识。

Dialogue:

Yibing: Alright, here we are!

Nicole: Wow, this is quite a nice factory. It looks really clean and well-organized.

Yibing: Thank you! We take a lot of pride in maintaining a clean and efficient workspace. Let me show you around. This way, please.

Nicole: OK.

Yibing: Nicole, I'd like to introduce you to Michael, our factory director. He oversees all of our production operations.

Nicole: Hi Michael, it's great to meet you!

Michael: Hello, Nicole! Welcome to visit our factory. I've heard a lot about your visit.

Yibing: And over here is Chris, our marketing director. He handles all our product launches and market strategies.

Chris: Hi Nicole, nice to finally put a face to the name. We've heard so much about your projects.

Nicole: Hi Chris, likewise! I'm really excited to see how everything operates here.

Yibing: And this is Amy, my assistant. She's been a huge help in organizing today's visit.

Amy: Hi Nicole, it's a pleasure to meet you. I've been following your work for some time now.

Nicole: Thanks, Amy! And thanks for all your hard work in setting this up. I really appreciate it.

Yibing: Oh, and here comes Mr. Zhang, our general manager. He's the man in charge!

Mr. Zhang: Nicole, welcome to our factory! I apologize for being late. I was caught up in another meeting, but I'm very happy you're here.

Nicole: No worries at all, Mr. Zhang! I've just been telling Yibing how impressed I am with the factory. It's so clean and organized, you can really tell a lot of care goes into the operations here.

Mr. Zhang: Thank you, Nicole! We believe a well-maintained factory reflects the quality of our work. We want to make sure everything runs smoothly from production to delivery.

Nicole: I can see that. It must take a lot of effort to keep everything this streamlined.

Mr. Zhang: It does, but we have a great team here. Michael and his staff do an excellent job of making sure we meet our production targets while keeping the quality high.

Nicole: That's great to hear. I always believe that a well-organized factory is key to ensuring reliable product quality. Honestly, it seems like a place I wouldn't mind working in myself!

Mr. Zhang: (laughing...) You're always welcome here, Nicole! We'd love to have you on board anytime.

Nicole: (laughing...) I'll keep that in mind! I'd love to know more about your production process. How many lines are you currently running?

Michael: We currently have five production lines, with the capacity to expand to seven during peak seasons. Each line is fully automated, which

helps us maintain consistency in quality.

Nicole: That's impressive! Automation must really help with efficiency. How long does it typically take to complete a production cycle for one batch?

Michael: For a standard product, it usually takes around two to three weeks to complete one full production cycle, depending on the complexity of the design. For larger or more customized orders, it can take up to five weeks.

Nicole: That's good to know. It sounds like you've got a solid system in place. I'd love to take a closer look at the production lines later.

Mr. Zhang: Absolutely. We'll give you a full tour so you can see every step of the process. I think you'll find it interesting, especially how we incorporate quality control at every stage.

Nicole: I'm looking forward to that. It's always fascinating to see how everything comes together on the factory floor.

参考译文

毅冰：好了，我们到啦。

Nicole：哇，这个工厂真不错。看起来非常干净，也很有条理。

毅冰：谢谢！我们非常注重保持干净、高效的工作环境。我带你四处参观一下。这边请。

Nicole：好的。

毅冰：Nicole，我来介绍一下，这是我们的厂长 Michael。他负责所有的生产运营工作。

Nicole：你好，Michael，很高兴见到你！

Michael：你好，Nicole！欢迎来到我们的工厂。我已经听说你要来了。

毅冰：这位是我们的市场总监 Chris。他负责所有的产品发布和市场策略。

Chris: 你好，Nicole，终于见到你了。我们听到很多关于你的项目。

Nicole: 你好，Chris！很高兴见到你！我真的很期待看看这里的运作情况。

毅冰: 这是我的助理 Amy。她在安排今天的参观行程上帮了很大的忙。

Amy: 你好，Nicole，很高兴见到你。我一直很关注你的工作。

Nicole: 谢谢你，Amy！也谢谢你为今天的安排所做的工作。我非常感激。

毅冰: 哦，还有那边走过来的是张先生，我们的总经理。他是这里的负责人！

张先生: Nicole，欢迎来到我们的工厂！抱歉我来晚了。刚才在开另一个会议，但非常高兴你能来。

Nicole: 没关系，张先生！我刚跟毅冰说，我对这个工厂印象非常深刻。这里非常干净、有序，可以看出大家对运营投入了很多精力。

张先生: 谢谢你，Nicole！我们相信，一个用心经营的工厂可以反映出我们的工作质量。我们希望从生产到交付，一切都能顺利进行。

Nicole: 我能看出来。这么高效的管理一定需要付出很多的努力来维持。

张先生: 是的，但我们有一个出色的团队。Michael 和他的员工们确保我们按时完成生产目标的同时保持着高质量。

Nicole: 听到这个真好。我一直认为，一个组织良好的工厂是确保产品质量可靠的关键。老实说，在这样的地方工作应该会很棒！

张先生:（笑）Nicole，你随时都可以来！我们随时欢迎你参观。

Nicole:（笑）我会记住的！我也很想了解更多关于你们的生产流程。你们目前有多少条生产线在运作？

Michael: 目前我们有五条生产线，在旺季时可以扩展到七条。每条生产线都是全自动化的，这有助于我们保持质量的稳定性。

Nicole: 这真让人印象深刻！自动化肯定大大提高了效率。完成一批订单的生产周期通常需要多长时间？

Michael: 对于标准产品，通常需要两到三周完成整个生产周期，具体取决于设计的复杂性。如果是较大或定制的订单，可能需要五周。

Nicole: 知道了，这很好。听起来你们有一套完美的系统。稍后我很想更仔细地看看生产线的运作情况。

张先生: 当然可以。我们会为你安排一次完整的参观，让你看到每个生产步骤。我想你会对我们如何在每个阶段融入质量控制感兴趣。

Nicole: 我非常期待。能亲眼看到工厂里的运作方式总是很有趣的。

Words & Phrases（词汇和句型）

well-organized 井井有条的、井然有序的

product launch 产品发布

put a face to the name 把脸和名字对应起来（表示见到真人）

the man in charge 负责人（非常口语化的表达）

from production to delivery 从生产到交付

Chinglish Correction（中式英语纠错）

笑死我了！

【Chinglish】

I'm happy and laughing!

【Native English】

You are killing me!

▶ 毅冰补充：

英文口语中，You are killing me! 是一个很常用的句型，表示"太好笑了！""笑死我了！"。

这个句型甚至可以省略主语和谓语，直接说"Killing me!"。这里绝对不是"杀了我"的意思，而是"太逗了""太搞笑了"。

18 客户来访，详细传递核心价值

故事背景

> 毅冰的老板张先生让毅冰先带 Nicole 到处转转，参观一下工厂，他自己有点事情要先处理一下，晚一点再过来。于是毅冰带路，厂长 Michael 和助理 Amy 陪同，带 Nicole 正式参观工厂。

Dialogue:

Mr. Zhang: Yibing, could you show Nicole around the factory for me? I've got to handle a few <u>urgent matters</u>, but I'll join you shortly. Mr. Johnson is waiting for my call.

Yibing: Of course, Mr. Zhang. I'll take care of it.

Mr. Zhang: Nicole, I apologize, but I have to <u>step away</u> for a bit. There's something pressing I need to deal with. Yibing will guide you on a quick tour of our production area.

Nicole: No problem at all, Mr. Zhang. Please take your time.

Mr. Zhang: Thanks for your understanding. I'll catch up with you later.

(They walk toward the workshop...)

Yibing: Alright, Nicole, this is our main <u>production workshop</u>. We've got ten injection molding machines and two blow molding machines here. The workers you see are handling the plastic components. We recently built new tooling for these parts.

Nicole: Interesting! By the way, which brand are your injection machines?

Yibing: Hmm, let me check on that. Michael, do you know the brand?

Michael: Yes, they're from LUST, a German brand. We imported them specifically for their precision and reliability. Have you heard of them?

Nicole: Oh, absolutely! LUST is well-known in the industry. You've got top-notch equipment here!

Yibing: Yes, we're really confident of our setup. It's made a big difference in maintaining high-quality standards.

Nicole: I can see that. And how many workers do you have in total?

Michael: We've got around 300 employees. About 50 are dedicated to production, 120 handle assembly, 60 are in charge of packaging, and the rest focus on quality control, material procurement, and various internal operations.

Nicole: That's a solid setup. Sounds like everything's well-organized.

Michael: We try to keep it efficient. Let's head upstairs so you can see our assembly line and packaging department. It'll give you a full picture of how we manage the workflow from start to finish.

Nicole: Sounds good. I'd love to see more.

参考译文 📖

张先生： 毅冰，你带 Nicole 在工厂转转吧。我这边还有些紧急的事情需要处理，稍后我会过来。Johnson 先生正在等我的电话。

毅冰： 没问题，张总。我会照顾好的。

张先生： Nicole，抱歉，我这边有些紧急的事情需要处理，可能要暂时离开一会儿。毅冰会带你参观我们的生产区域。

Nicole： 完全没问题，张先生。你先忙。

张先生： 谢谢你的理解。稍后我过来找你。

（他们走向车间……）

毅冰：好的，Nicole，这里是我们的主要生产车间。我们有 10 台注塑机和 2 台吹塑机。你看到的这些工人正在制作塑料零件。最近我们为这些零件新建了模具。

Nicole：很有意思！顺便问一下，你们的注塑机是什么品牌？

毅冰：嗯，我不太确定，得问一下。Michael，你知道是什么品牌吗？

Michael：是的，是 LUST 品牌的，来自德国。我们一直使用这些机器，主要看重它们的精度和可靠性。你听说过这个品牌吗？

Nicole：哇，当然听过！LUST 在业内很有名。你们的设备真的是顶级的！

毅冰：是的，我们对这些设备非常有信心。它们在保证高质量标准方面起了很大作用。

Nicole：我能看得出来。那么你们工厂一共有多少工人？

Michael：我们大约有 300 名员工。大约 50 人负责生产，120 人负责组装，60 人负责包装，剩下的负责质量控制、物料采购以及一些内部运营。

Nicole：这个布局很好。听起来你们的管理很有条理。

Michael：我们尽量保持高效运作。我们去楼上看看我们的组装线和包装部门吧。这样你就能更全面地了解从生产到交付的整个流程。

Nicole：听起来不错。我很想看看更多的东西。

Words & Phrases（词汇和句型）

urgent matter 紧急事项（something pressing 也是这个意思）

step away 这里表示"稍稍离开一下"

production workshop 生产车间

top-notch 顶级的

assembly 组装、装配

Chinglish Correction（中式英语纠错）

针对客户来访，事先准备很关键！

【Chinglish】

Concerning clients' visiting, the preparation is very important!

【Native English】

The preparation is crucial to seal the deal with clients.

▶ **毅冰补充：**

　　这句话需要避免直译，要拎出主干，把"事先准备"作为主语，然后表达"关键就是搞定客户"。客户来访的目的是什么？准备的目的是什么？就是为了做生意，就是为了寻找合作机会，就是为了让客户满意。那准备的目的出来了，就是"搞定客户"，就可以用一个专门的短语 seal the deal with somebody，表示"搞定某人"。

19　实景谈判，如何有效展示优势

故事背景 ✏

　　看完工厂后，毅冰带 Nicole 去了会议室，大家坐下来交换意见。这时候，Nicole 对工厂已经有了初步认知，接下来自然要进入具体的项目和相关的谈判。这个时候，才是真正意义上的实景谈判。

Dialogue:

Yibing: So, what do you think?

Nicole: It looks pretty good overall.

Yibing: Thank you, I'm glad you think so!

Nicole: But I'd like to learn more about your company. I noticed some items in your warehouse with METRO's shipping mark on them.

Yibing: Yes, that's correct.

Nicole: Do you work directly with METRO, or through importers?

Yibing: Sorry, could you clarify?

Nicole: I mean, are you working directly with METRO in Germany, or do you get the orders through other trading companies?

Yibing: Oh, we work directly with METRO's Hong Kong office. The goods are eventually shipped to Hamburg or Bremerhaven in Germany. METRO Hong Kong is their Asia-Pacific sourcing hub, and it operates under their headquarters in Germany.

Nicole: I see. That makes sense. Could you show me some of the items you supply to them?

Yibing: Sure, but I can only show you a few of the open-mold items. Some of their products are private molds, so we have to keep those confidential due to the agreement we have with them.

Nicole: I completely understand. Do you handle other private label projects as well?

Yibing: Yes, we do. Besides METRO, we manage private label production for several other major retailers across Europe. Each project is tailored to the client's specifications, from design to final delivery.

Nicole: That's great. I'm always impressed by companies that can handle both standard and customized production. It shows flexibility.

Yibing: Absolutely! It's all about understanding the client's needs and delivering the right solution, whether it's an open-mold product or a fully customized design.

参考译文 📖

毅冰： 你觉得怎么样？

Nicole： 总的来说，感觉挺不错的。

毅冰： 谢谢，很高兴你这么认为！

Nicole： 但我还想多了解一下你们公司。我在你们仓库里看到一些带有麦德龙品牌唛头的货物。

毅冰： 是的，没错。

Nicole： 你们是直接和麦德龙合作，还是通过进口商？

毅冰： 不好意思，你能再解释一下吗？

Nicole： 我的意思是，你们是和德国的麦德龙直接合作，还是通过其他贸易公司拿到订单的？

毅冰： 哦，我们是和麦德龙的香港办公室直接合作，货物最终会发往德国的汉堡或不来梅港。麦德龙香港是他们亚太区的采购中心，隶属于德国总部。

Nicole： 明白了，合情合理。你可以展示一下你们给他们供货的产品吗？

毅冰： 当然，不过我只能给你展示一些公开模具的产品，因为其他的是他们的私有模具产品，基于保密协议，我们不能公开。

Nicole： 我完全理解。你们也做一些其他品牌的项目吗？

毅冰： 是的，我们有。除了麦德龙之外，我们还为欧洲的几家大型零售商安排贴牌生产。每个项目都是根据客户的具体要求量身定制的，从设计到最终交付。

Nicole： 太棒了。我总是对那些能够同时处理标准化和定制化生产的公司印象深刻，说明你们非常灵活。

毅冰： 当然！这关键在于理解客户的需求，并提供合适的解决方案，不管是公开模具产品还是完全定制化的设计。

Words & Phrases（词汇和句型）

shipping mark 唛头（侧唛是 side mark）

Asia-Pacific sourcing hub 亚太区采购中心

open-mold items 公模产品（相对应，私模产品是 private-mold items）

major retailers 主要零售商

customized production 定制化生产

Chinglish Correction（中式英语纠错）

能不能填一下附件的报价单?

【Chinglish】

Could you fill the attached offer sheet?

【Native English】

Could you fill the attached offer sheet out?

▶ **毅冰补充:**

这里，fill the offer sheet out 是一个固定搭配，表示"填报价单"，这个 out 是不能省略的。日常工作中，很多客户有自己的报价单，会发过来让供应商填写，业务员一旦完成后，回复客户邮件或者与客户通电话时，随意来一句 I have filled the offer sheet out in your format（我已经根据你的格式填好报价单），绝对会让客户刮目相看的。

20 安排送行，也不能出现冷场

故事背景

> Nicole 终于完成了拜访任务，准备回酒店休息，然后第二天再继续她的商务行程。毅冰提前安排好了车，陪 Nicole 一起过去，在路上可以顺便聊几句。对方千里迢迢来中国，机会难得，借此机会怎么都要混个脸熟，给对方更深刻的印象才行。

Dialogue:

Nicole: Thanks so much for your time today, Yibing!

Yibing: Oh, don't mention it! It was my pleasure. Honestly, I should be the one thanking you for taking the time to visit us. I really hope we can get some business going soon.

Nicole: I'm sure we will.

Yibing: So, is this your first time in Shanghai?

Nicole: No, I've actually been here quite a few times over the past seven years.

Yibing: Ah, I see. Mostly for business, or do you sneak in some <u>sightseeing</u> too?

Nicole: Honestly? Mostly business. It's usually just visiting suppliers, placing orders, negotiating prices, fixing problems—you know, all the fun stuff. Not a whole lot of time to play tourist.

Yibing: (laughing...) Yeah, I get it. Sounds like you're always <u>on the go</u>.

Nicole: Oh, for sure. There's always something to handle.

Yibing: How are things in Europe these days, business-wise? I've been hearing the economy's been a bit rough over there.

Nicole: Yeah, you're right.

Yibing: And what about Germany? Things any better there?

Nicole: Germany's holding up, but just barely. It's stable, but far from booming.

Yibing: Yikes, that's a pretty <u>heavy conversation</u>!

Nicole: Yeah, definitely not the most uplifting topic. Let's change gears—how about we grab a coffee at my hotel and unwind a bit?

Yibing: That sounds perfect. I could definitely use a break.

Nicole: Awesome, let's do it. I know a great little spot at the hotel where we can relax and chat some more.

Yibing: <u>Lead the way!</u>

参考译文 📖

Nicole：毅冰，今天非常感谢你抽出时间！

毅冰： 嗨，别客气！这是我的荣幸。说实话，我应该感谢你特地来访问我们。我真的希望我们能尽快开展合作。

Nicole：我相信我们会的。

毅冰： 你是第一次来上海吗？

Nicole：不，其实这七年来我已经来了好几次了。

毅冰： 噢，我懂了。大部分都是出差吗？还是偶尔有时间可以四处看看？

Nicole：说实话，基本都是出差。通常就是拜访供应商、下订单、谈价格、解决问题——你懂的，都是这些"有趣"的事。没什么时间当游客。

毅冰：（笑）啊，我明白了。听起来你总是忙得团团转。

Nicole：没错。总有些事情要处理。

毅冰：那欧洲这几年生意怎么样？我听说经济情况有点糟糕。

Nicole：是啊，你说得对。

毅冰：那德国怎么样？那边情况好点吗？

Nicole：德国还算撑得住，但也只是勉强维持。经济稳定，离"繁荣"还远。

毅冰：哇，这话题真有点沉重啊！

Nicole：是啊，确实不怎么让人振奋。换个话题吧——咱们去酒店喝杯咖啡，放松一下，怎么样？

毅冰：听起来不错。我也确实需要休息一下。

Nicole：太好了，那就这么定了。我知道酒店里有个不错的小咖啡厅，我们可以边喝边聊。

毅冰：那你带路吧！

Words & Phrases（词汇和句型）

sightseeing 观光、游览

on the go 忙忙碌碌、四处奔走

heavy conversation 沉重的谈话

Lead the way! 你来带路！（口语中很常见，譬如朋友说某个餐厅很棒，是新开的网红店，你就可以来这句，让他带路。）

Chinglish Correction（中式英语纠错）

你的建议太好了！

【Chinglish】

What a good idea!

【Native English】

What a terrific idea!

毅冰补充：

在这里，terrific 的程度就比 good 要强很多，是 wonderful 的近义词，但是更加通俗化，能让客户觉得你英文用词很灵活，非常地道。

21 咖啡厅闲聊，拉近交情的必要动作

故事背景

> 毅冰送 Nicole 回到酒店后，发现一楼的大堂吧很多人，没有空位，就出门在附近找了一家咖啡厅。一线江景，直面黄浦江，正适合三两朋友闲聊，顺便喝点东西。毅冰过去点单，Nicole 入乡随俗，想要抢着买单。

Dialogue:

Yibing: Amazing view, right? You can really feel the fresh air, and the Huangpu River looks so beautiful from here.

Nicole: Yeah, it's a really <u>nice spot</u>.

Yibing: I'll go grab the coffees. What can I get for you? You want an <u>espresso</u>?

Nicole: No, thanks. I'm more into something sweeter—how about a Caramel Macchiato?

Yibing: Interesting! Most of my German customers are all about the strong stuff, like espresso. Some of them even order <u>double shots</u>.

Nicole: (laughing...) I know, but I'm the exception. I prefer <u>milder</u>

drinks. I'm more into lattes, cappuccinos, and anything that's not too bitter.

Yibing: Got it! One Caramel Macchiato coming right up. Do you want a Grande or Venti?

Nicole: Actually, a Tall will do. I'm trying not to overdo it on caffeine today.

Yibing: (smiling...) Fair enough. Anything to eat? Maybe a croissant, cheesecake, or a muffin?

Nicole: I'll pass for now, thanks. What about you? What's your go-to?

Yibing: I'm getting a Cranberry White Chocolate Mocha with extra whipped cream, Venti-sized, of course. And I might treat myself to a Black Forest muffin too.

Nicole: Black Forest, like Schwarzwald?

Yibing: Yeah, wait... what does that mean?

Nicole: It's German! Schwarz means black, and Wald means forest. So, Schwarzwald is literally Black Forest. The cake's named after the region in Germany.

Yibing: Ahh, that makes sense! Thanks for the German lesson!

Nicole: (laughing...) Anytime! So, how much is it? I'll get this round.

Yibing: Oh no, please, it's on me. You've had a long day—let me treat you.

Nicole: Seriously, Yibing, you've been so helpful today. It's only fair that I pay.

Yibing: Tell you what—next time when I'm in Germany, the coffee's on you. Sound good?

Nicole: Deal! And when you visit, I'll make sure you try some real Black Forest cake from the actual Schwarzwald.

Yibing: Now that's an offer I can't refuse!

参考译文 📖

毅冰： 景色不错，对吧？空气很清新，而且从这里看黄浦江特别美。

Nicole： 是啊，真是个好地方。

毅冰： 我去拿咖啡，你想喝什么？意式浓缩？

Nicole： 不用了，谢谢。我更喜欢甜一点的咖啡——给我来杯焦糖玛奇朵吧。

毅冰： 有意思！我很多德国客户都喜欢喝浓咖啡，像意式浓缩。有些人甚至要双份的。

Nicole：（笑）我知道，但我是个例外。我更喜欢淡一点的，像拿铁、卡布奇诺，或者其他不那么苦的咖啡。

毅冰： 明白了！那就一杯焦糖玛奇朵。要大杯还是超大杯？

Nicole： 其实中杯就够了。今天不想喝太多咖啡。

毅冰：（笑）说得对。要吃点什么吗？牛角可颂面包、芝士蛋糕，还是松饼？

Nicole： 现在不用了，谢谢。你呢？你一般点什么？

毅冰： 我会来一杯蔓越莓白巧克力摩卡，加双倍奶油，当然是最大杯的。顺便再加一个黑森林松饼。

Nicole： 黑森林，像 Schwarzwald？

毅冰： 是的，等等……那是什么意思？

Nicole： 这是德语！Schwarz 是"黑色"，Wald 是"森林"。所以 Schwarzwald 就是"黑森林"。这种蛋糕就是以德国的黑森林地区命名的。

毅冰： 啊，明白了！谢谢你的德语小课堂！

Nicole：（笑）随时欢迎！多少钱？这次我来请吧。

毅冰： 哦，不用，我请。这是我的心意，你今天忙了一天，放松一下吧。

Nicole： 真的，毅冰，今天你帮了我很多忙。应该我请。

毅冰： 这样吧，下次我去德国的时候，你请我喝咖啡。怎么样？

Nicole：成交！等你来的时候，我一定带你去尝尝真正的黑森林蛋糕，直接从黑森林地区来的。

毅冰：这个提议我可拒绝不了！

Words & Phrases（词汇和句型）

nice spot 好地方（一般情况下多用于观景点）

espresso 意式浓缩咖啡（大量欧洲客户的偏好）

double shots 双份浓度

milder drinks 温和的饮料

overdo 过度、过多、过火

Chinglish Correction（中式英语纠错）

他是一个阅历丰富的人。

【Chinglish】

He is a man with full of knowledge and experience.

【Native English】

He is a man of the world.

▶ **毅冰补充：**

不要从字面上去直接翻译。阅历丰富，好像是有很多的知识，有很多的经历，就容易译成 full of knowledge and experience。

其实英语有一个地道的表达，a man of the world，是一个固定搭配，就是用来表示"阅历丰富的人""见过山和大海的人"。

22 预约后续行程，增加最后一个闪光点

故事背景

> 毅冰和 Nicole 在咖啡厅喝东西，闲聊了一会儿，随即送她回酒店休息。两人在大堂简单聊了下行程和后续的接送安排。

Dialogue:

Yibing: So, what's on your agenda for tomorrow? Meeting with any other suppliers?

Nicole: Yeah, I've got one more meeting in the Qingpu district here in Shanghai. They're a potential new supplier, so I'm looking forward to seeing what they offer.

Yibing: That's exciting! Qingpu's a bit out of the way, though. Are they handling transportation for you, or would you like us to arrange something?

Nicole: Thanks for offering, but they've got it covered. I'll be fine. However, I could definitely use your help getting to the airport the day after tomorrow.

Yibing: Absolutely, no problem at all. What time is your flight?

Nicole: Let me check... It's at 1:05 p.m. from Pudong Airport.

Yibing: Alright. Since it can take around an hour to get to the airport, maybe we should leave the hotel around 10:00 a.m.? That should give us enough <u>buffer time</u>, just in case traffic is bad.

Nicole: That sounds perfect. I trust your judgment. Traffic here can be <u>unpredictable</u>, right?

Yibing: Definitely. Sometimes it's smooth, and other times it's a nightmare, especially around Pudong. Better safe than sorry. I'll plan to meet you in the lobby at 9:30 a.m., just to give us a bit of <u>extra cushion</u>.

Nicole: That works for me. I'll be ready. And I'll make sure to check out of the hotel <u>beforehand</u> so there are no delays.

Yibing: Great! I'll double-check everything on my end too. If you need anything else, feel free to let me know before then. Oh, and how was your room, by the way? I hope everything's been comfortable during your stay.

Nicole: Oh, it's been great, thank you for asking! The hotel's been wonderful, and the staff is super helpful. Honestly, I couldn't have asked for a better place to stay.

Yibing: I'm glad to hear that. It's always nice when things go smoothly. And it sounds like everything's all set for your final meetings tomorrow, so you should be good to go.

Nicole: Yeah, I'm wrapping things up pretty well. Just one more supplier to meet, then I can <u>head back home</u>.

Yibing: I'm sure you're ready to get home after all this traveling.

Nicole: You have no idea! But I've had a productive trip, so I can't complain.

Yibing: That's the best feeling, getting everything done and then heading home. Alright, I'll see you at 9:30 on departure day. Safe travels with tomorrow's meeting!

Nicole: Thanks, Yibing. I appreciate all your help. See you soon!

参考译文 📖

毅冰: 那么，明天你的行程是怎么安排的？还会见其他供应商吗？

Nicole: 是的，明天我还有一个在上海青浦区的会面。他们是一个潜在的新供应商，我很期待看看他们能提供什么。

毅冰：听起来很有意思！不过青浦有点远。他们安排好交通了吗？还是需要我们帮你安排？

Nicole：谢谢你的提议，但他们已经安排好了。我没问题的。不过后天去机场的事，可能需要你帮忙了。

毅冰：当然，没问题！你的航班是几点的？

Nicole：让我查一下……是下午 1:05，从浦东机场起飞。

毅冰：好的。去机场通常要一个小时，我们大概上午 10 点从酒店出发？这样能留出一些时间缓冲，以防堵车。

Nicole：这听起来很合适。我相信你的判断。这里的交通确实有点难以预料，对吧？

毅冰：没错。有时候很顺畅，但有时候简直是噩梦，尤其是去浦东机场的路上。多留点时间总没坏处。我计划 9:30 在酒店大堂等你，这样我们有更多的时间可以应对。

Nicole：听起来不错。我到时会准备好的。我会提前办好退房手续，以免耽误时间。

毅冰：好的！我这边也会再确认所有安排。如果你有其他需要，随时告诉我。哦，对了，房间住得怎么样？希望你这次住得舒服。

Nicole：太好了，谢谢你的关心！酒店非常棒，员工也很贴心、热情。老实说，我找不到比这里更好的地方了。

毅冰：听你这么说我很开心。事情顺利总是好事。看起来你明天的最后一个会议也安排好了，应该一切顺利。

Nicole：是的，我基本上都处理得差不多了。再见一个供应商就可以回家了。

毅冰：我相信你肯定已经准备好回家了，毕竟出了这么久的差。

Nicole：你说得没错！不过这次行程很有成效，所以也不能抱怨什么。

毅冰：完成所有任务，然后回家，那真是最好的感觉了。好吧，出发那天上午 9:30 见。祝你明天的会面顺利！

　　Nicole：谢谢你，毅冰。非常感谢你的帮助。回头见！

Words & Phrases（词汇和句型）

buffer time 缓冲时间、机动时间

unpredictable 不可预测的、无法预见的

extra cushion 额外的靠垫（这里指额外的缓冲时间）

beforehand 事先、提前、预先（相当于 in advance）

head back home 回家

Chinglish Correction（中式英语纠错）

请给我一杯大杯的香草拿铁，打包带走。

【Chinglish】

Please give me a big cup of Vanilla Latte, and take it away.

【Native English】

Grande Vanilla Latte to go, please.

▶ **毅冰补充：**

　　英语口语中，是不需要逐字逐句去翻译的。在英语国家，在描述的名词后面简单地加一个 to go，就表示"打包""带走"的意思。grande 是意大利语的翻译，在咖啡店里就是"大杯"的意思，大家都能听懂。

业务细节谈判，
拒绝中式英语

23 样品间的介绍，展示公司实力特点

故事背景

意大利客户 Fernando 先生第一次来毅冰公司拜访，大致参观工厂后，就回到样品间准备开会。会议一开始，Fernando 就要求毅冰做一下公司介绍，让他先有个大致的了解。

Dialogue:

Yibing: Alright, Mr. Fernando, let me start with a quick introduction about our company. I've prepared a <u>brief presentation</u>, which you can follow along with on the <u>projector</u> here.

Mr. Fernando: Sounds good.

Yibing: So, our company was founded in 1988, giving us full of experience in the lighting industry. Back then, we started with a small factory and only 20 staff members. Our annual sales were around $13000 at the time. But over the past <u>couple of decades</u>, we've seen tremendous growth. Today, we have 300 workers in our factory and another 50 staff members across different teams in our trading company.

Mr. Fernando: That's impressive.

Yibing: Thank you! And our business continues to grow. Last year, our sales turnover reached $10 million, largely driven by our solar lights and other lighting products.

Mr. Fernando: Wow, that's great.

Yibing: Yes, and our products are now sold across the globe. Some of our key markets include the US, Germany, Canada, France, the UK, Sweden, Japan, the Netherlands, and Belgium.

Mr. Fernando: What's the breakdown of your orders from Europe, percentage-wise?

Yibing: About 65% of our orders come from Europe, 15% from the US, and the remaining 20% from other countries or regions.

Mr. Fernando: Interesting. And what about Italy specifically? Do you have a significant share from the Italian market?

Yibing: To be honest, we currently don't have any direct customers in Italy. However, we do work with a lot of importers in the Netherlands and Belgium, so it's possible that some of our products are being sold in Italy through those channels.

Mr. Fernando: Well, I might just be your first direct customer in Italy, then.

Yibing: We'd love that! We're always excited to expand into new markets. Let me show you this chart—this highlights our turnover growth and current market share. On the next slide, you'll see a list of our testing certificates and reports, which will give you a clearer picture of our product quality and standards.

Mr. Fernando: That's exactly what I was looking for. I'm particularly interested in the certifications you have.

Yibing: I'm glad to hear that. We take quality control very seriously, and we've ensured that all our products meet the highest industry standards. We've got certifications like CE, RoHS, and ETL for various markets. If you need further details, I can send you the full report as well.

Mr. Fernando: That would be great. I'm looking forward to reviewing those in detail.

Yibing: Absolutely. I'll have those sent over to you right after our meeting. If you have any specific questions or need further clarification, just let me know!

参考译文 📖

毅冰：好，Fernando 先生，我先简单介绍一下我们公司。我准备了一份简短的演示，你可以通过投影仪跟着一起看。

Fernando 先生：听起来不错。

毅冰：我们公司成立于 1988 年，在照明行业有丰富的经验。最初，我们只有一个小工厂，员工只有 20 人。当时的年销售额大约为 13000 美元。但在过去的几十年里，我们取得了巨大的进步。如今，我们的自有工厂有 300 名员工，贸易公司还有 50 名员工分布在不同的团队中。

Fernando 先生：这令人印象十分深刻。

毅冰：谢谢！而且我们的业务量还在持续增长。去年我们的销售额达到了 1000 万美元，主要依靠我们的太阳能灯和其他照明产品。

Fernando 先生：哇，真不错。

毅冰：是的，而且我们的产品现在销往全球。我们的主要市场包括美国、德国、加拿大、法国、英国、瑞典、日本、荷兰和比利时。

Fernando 先生：那你们欧洲订单的比例大概是多少？

毅冰：大约 65% 的订单来自欧洲，15% 来自美国，剩下的 20% 来自其他国家或地区。

Fernando 先生：有意思。那么具体到意大利呢？你们在意大利的市场份额大吗？

毅冰：说实话，目前我们还没有来自意大利的直接客户。但是我们与荷兰和比利时的许多进口商合作，所以我们的产品可能通过这些渠道在意大利销售。

Fernando 先生：那么，我可能就是你们在意大利的第一个直接客户了。

毅冰：我们非常期待！我们总是很兴奋能进入新的市场。让我给你展示一下这张图表——它展示了我们的销售增长和当前的市场份额。在下一页，你可以看到我们获得的测试认证和报告列表，这将让你更清楚地了解我们产品的质量和标准。

Fernando 先生：这正是我想了解的。我特别关注你们获得的认证。

毅冰：我很高兴你感兴趣。我们非常重视质量控制，并确保所有产品都符合最高的行业标准。我们有像 CE、RoHS 和 ETL 等各种市场的认证。如果你需要更详细的资料，我可以把完整的报告发给你。

Fernando 先生：那太好了。我很期待仔细看看这些报告。

毅冰：没问题。会后我会把这些资料发给你。如果你有任何具体问题或需要进一步的说明，请随时告诉我！

Words & Phrases（词汇和句型）

brief presentation 简明扼要的演讲

projector 投影仪

couple of decades 几十年（一般用于表示二三十年）

turnover growth 销售额增长

current market share 当前市场份额

Chinglish Correction（中式英语纠错）

别计较了，赶紧做好公司简介发过去吧。

【Chinglish】

Don't worry, please do the company introduction and send it out asap.

【Native English】

Be that as it may, do the company presentation and send it out asap.

▶ **毅冰补充：**

"别计较了"，可以用 be that as it may 这个短语，比大而化之的 don't worry 更加细化，更能突出说话者的心理变化。

24 现场即时报价，精确掌握谈判艺术

故事背景

Fernando 先生在样品间里四处参观，毅冰在一旁做简要的介绍，回答一些专业的问题。对于 Fernando 挑中的样品，毅冰示意可以先放在地上，回头再一并整理资料发给他。

Dialogue:

Yibing: This is one of our newest products, specifically developed for the European market.

Mr. Fernando: Who have you sold it to so far?

Yibing: Not yet. We're planning to launch it at the Canton Fair next spring.

Mr. Fernando: Got it. And what's the price point?

Yibing: It depends on the order quantity. If you're able to place an order for a full 20-foot container, we can offer a price of USD 3.74 per unit.

Mr. Fernando: How many units can fit into a 20-foot container?

Yibing: 8000 pieces, <u>give or take</u>.

Mr. Fernando: That's quite a lot. We're only looking at around 500 to 1000 units for a trial order.

Yibing: I see. In that case, we'll have to discuss the pricing later based on the smaller volume.

Mr. Fernando: Of course. What about this other product here?

Yibing: Oh, for this model, we received an order from Aldi last year for 1 million units.

Mr. Fernando: Wow, so you must have really competitive pricing on this one, right?

Yibing: We believe so, and we're confident in our pricing. But I'll need to know your order quantity before I can provide a <u>final offer</u>.

Mr. Fernando: Same issue. We'll likely start with a smaller quantity. Could you place both this item and the previous one on the <u>boardroom</u> table so we can review them later?

Yibing: No worries, I'll set them aside for now. We can gather everything for your final review after you've had a chance to think it over.

Mr. Fernando: Sounds good. Let's keep moving.

Yibing: Over here on this shelf, you'll find our promotional items for the US market. All of them come in double blister packaging and include Ni-Cd batteries.

Mr. Fernando: Let's skip those for now.

Yibing: No problem. And here are our one-dollar lights, packaged in <u>display boxes</u>.

Mr. Fernando: Are there different color options available?

Yibing: Absolutely. We can customize the colors based on your needs. Would you like to set one of these aside as well for later review?

Mr. Fernando: Sure, why not.

参考译文 📖

毅冰： 这是我们最新开发的产品，专门为欧洲市场设计的。

Fernando 先生： 到目前为止，你们卖给谁了？

毅冰： 还没有。我们计划在明年春季的广交会上正式推出。

Fernando 先生： 明白了。价格是多少？

毅冰： 价格取决于订单数量。如果你能订一个 20 英尺集装箱的数量，我们可以提供每件 3.74 美元的价格。

Fernando 先生： 20 尺柜能装多少件？

毅冰： 大约 8000 件。

Fernando 先生： 这数量挺大的。我们现在只想先试订单，大概 500 到 1000 件。

毅冰： 我明白了。那我们回头可以根据较小的数量来讨论价格。

Fernando 先生： 没问题。那么这款产品呢？

毅冰： 哦，这款产品去年我们收到 Aldi 的订单，数量是 100 万件。

Fernando 先生： 哇，那这款的价格肯定很有竞争力吧？

毅冰： 确实，我们对这个价格也很有信心。不过我需要知道你的订购数量，才能给出最终报价。

Fernando 先生： 还是同样的问题。我们可能会从较小的数量开始。你能把这个和前面的那个产品放在会议室的桌子上吗？稍后我们逐一讨论。

毅冰： 没问题，我先把它们放在一边。稍后你有时间再确认时，我们会帮你都整理好。

Fernando 先生： 好的。那我们继续看其他产品吧。

毅冰： 这边的货架上，是我们为美国市场做的促销产品。它们都是双层吸塑包装，配有镍镉电池。

Fernando 先生： 这些我们暂时先跳过吧。

毅冰： 没问题。这里是我们的一美元灯，包装是展示盒形式的。

Fernando 先生：颜色可以选择吗？

毅冰：当然可以。我们可以根据你的需求定制颜色。你需要把这一款也放到一边稍后再看吗？

Fernando 先生：当然，为什么不呢？

Words & Phrases（词汇和句型）

so far 迄今为止、到目前为止

give or take 大约、左右

final offer 最终报价（相对应，"初步报价"是 initial offer）

boardroom 会议室

display box 展示盒（很多客户会表达成 PDQ）

Chinglish Correction（中式英语纠错）

这些是我们的老产品。

【Chinglish】

Here are our old items.

【Native English】

Here are our regular items.

毅冰补充：

千万不要想当然地把"老产品"翻译成 old items。如果这样说，那就是自己把生意往外推。客户一听到你这么说，就认为你在告诉他，"别买这些东西了，这都是一些过时的产品"。

正确的、地道的表达，应该是 regular items，表示这些是常规产品，是老产品，是已经成熟的产品，而不是那些刚开发的、未得到市场和消费者认可的新品。这也是英语和汉语之间的一个重大差异。

25 细化选中的样品，讨论价格和相关细节

故事背景

Fernando 先生走了一圈，选了 6 款产品。毅冰收集起来，拿到会议桌那边，一款一款地跟 Fernando 确认，讨论价格和相关细节。做一个初步的商讨后，双方交换意见。

Dialogue:

Yibing: Here they are—the six items you selected. Does everything look correct?

Mr. Fernando: Yes, that's right.

Yibing: Great. Let's start with the first one—our new model RJK-23366. For a 20-foot container, the unit price is USD 3.74 per piece. However, if you want to place a smaller trial order of 500 to 1000 pieces, we'd need to add an extra handling charge of USD 200.

Mr. Fernando: That's going to be tough. You have to understand, this is a brand-new item. We have no idea if the Italian market will respond positively or not. We need to test the waters, get feedback from the chain stores, and see how consumers react. Both of us need to share the risk—it's not fair for me to shoulder all of it.

Yibing: I understand. What would you suggest?

Mr. Fernando: Keep the price at USD 3.74 but let us start with a smaller quantity for the trial. I know your margins are tight, and believe me, mine are too. But if the product is a success, we'll both have the chance to benefit in the long run. I'm confident that if it performs well, I'll be placing much larger orders soon.

Yibing: I hear you, and I'm open to making this work. The challenge we face is in mass production. The production process for 1000 pieces is almost the same as for 10000 pieces, which drives up the cost and administrative overhead for smaller orders.

Mr. Fernando: I get that. Let's put that discussion on hold for now and come back to it later.

Yibing: Sure, that works.

Mr. Fernando: Now, about the price for this second item, the one you've supplied to Aldi—what can you offer me?

Yibing: Are we talking about the same color box packaging?

Mr. Fernando: Yes, and I'm thinking of ordering around 3000 pieces.

Yibing: Alright, for that quantity, we can offer USD 1.95 per piece.

Mr. Fernando: That's a bit <u>steep</u>. I was hoping for something below USD 1.80.

Yibing: I'm afraid that's going to be difficult. USD 1.90 is the best we can do.

Mr. Fernando: Alright, that works. Let's move on to the next one. I need pricing for 2000 pieces.

Yibing: You're referring to the colorful solar lights in display boxes, correct?

Mr. Fernando: Yes. How many pieces come in a set?

Yibing: We can pack either 24 or 48 pieces per set—it's your choice.

Mr. Fernando: I think 12 pieces per set would be better. Could you create a new display box size to accommodate that?

Yibing: Of course, but I'll need to recheck the pricing since the packaging cost will be a bit higher for the smaller box.

Mr. Fernando: Sounds good. My assistant will send over the die-cut design for the new box dimensions.

Yibing: Perfect, thank you! Now, for the next item—let's talk about the mini keychain LED light for promotional purposes...

参考译文 📖

毅冰：这是你刚刚选的 6 款产品，都对吗？

Fernando 先生：是的，没错。

毅冰：好的。我们先讨论第一个产品——我们的新型号 RJK-23366。对于一个 20 英尺集装箱的数量，单价是每件 3.74 美元。不过，如果你想先下 500 到 1000 件的试订单，我们需要收取 200 美元的额外操作费。

Fernando 先生：这有点难办。你得理解，这是一个全新的产品。我们完全不知道意大利市场是如何反应。我们需要测试市场，从连锁店获取反馈，看看消费者的反应。需要我们双方共同承担风险，不应该让我方承担所有风险。

毅冰：我理解。那你的建议是？

Fernando 先生：保持 3.74 美元的价格，但让我们这次能下小批量订单试水。我知道你的利润空间很小，我的也一样。但如果产品成功了，未来我们都有机会赚得更多。如果市场反应良好，我肯定会下更大的订单。

毅冰：我理解你的立场，也愿意作出调整。我们面临的挑战是大批量的生产。生产 1000 件的工作流程和生产 1 万件几乎一样，这意味着小订单的额外成本和管理费用要高得多。

Fernando 先生：我明白。那我们先把这个问题放一放，稍后讨论。

毅冰：好的，没问题。

Fernando 先生：那关于第二个产品，也就是你们供应给 Aldi 的那个，价格怎么样？

毅冰：是一样的彩盒包装吗？

Fernando 先生：是的，我打算订 3000 件左右。

毅冰：好的，这个数量的话，我们可以提供每件 1.95 美元的价格。

Fernando 先生：这有点贵。我希望能低于 1.80 美元。

毅冰：这恐怕有点困难。1.90 美元是我们能提供的最低价格了。

Fernando 先生：好吧，能接受。继续下一个产品吧。我需要 2000 件的报价。

毅冰：你说的是彩色太阳能灯，带展示盒的对吗？

Fernando 先生：是的。每套包含多少件？

毅冰：我们可以装 24 件或 48 件，取决于你选择哪种包装。

Fernando 先生：我觉得 12 件一套更合适。你们能为我们制作新的展示盒尺寸吗？

毅冰：当然可以，不过我需要重新核算价格，因为这种小尺寸的包装成本会稍微高一些。

Fernando 先生：好的。我的助理会把新的展示盒尺寸的刀模设计发给你们。

毅冰：完美，感谢！接下来我们讨论一下迷你钥匙扣 LED 灯的促销方案……

Words & Phrases（词汇和句型）

handling charge 操作费

brand-new item 新品

test the waters 试水（表示"测试市场反馈"）

chain stores 连锁门店

steep 难以接受的、过高的（这里表示"价格高"）

Chinglish Correction（中式英语纠错）

这个订单，我们的利润非常低！

【Chinglish】

Our profit is very low in this order!

【Native English】

Our margin is very thin in this order!

▶ **毅冰补充：**

表示利润低，可以用 low profit 来表示，语法没错，意思也没错，但是美国人往往不这样说。他们在口语和电邮里，还是经常用 margin 这个词来表示利润，用 thin 来表示"低""少"。

26 针对客户疑虑，策略与方案的再设计

故事背景

其他几款产品都谈判完毕后，大家又回到一开始有争议的第一款太阳能灯。Fernando 先生希望下小单，但是维持大货的价格；而毅冰要求对方增加订单数量，或者接受略高的价格。双方继续交换意见，争取达成一致。

Dialogue:

Yibing: Alright, let's circle back to the first item we discussed.

Mr. Fernando: Sure. If you agree with my suggestion, I think we're all set.

Yibing: Honestly, Mr. Fernando, you've put me in a bit of a tough spot here.

Mr. Fernando: Come on, it's not that tough—just help us out as we work to grow the market. That's all I'm asking!

Yibing: My boss is going to have my head for this! The best I can do on the handling fee is USD 150. That's really my final offer.

Mr. Fernando: I'll tell you what—I can <u>bump up</u> the order to 1200 pieces. But please, keep the price at USD 3.74 and drop the handling fee altogether.

Yibing: Give me just a moment. I need to double-check this.

Mr. Fernando: Take your time.

Yibing: I've checked, and the best I can do is USD 3.82 per piece. That's my <u>final number</u>.

Mr. Fernando: Come on, can we just round it to USD 3.80?

Yibing: (laughing...) Alright, <u>you got me!</u> USD 3.80 it is—for my VIP customer!

Mr. Fernando: Much appreciated! You've got yourself a deal.

参考译文 📖

毅冰： 好的，我们回到我们刚刚讨论的第一个产品。

Fernando 先生： 没问题。如果你同意我的建议，我想我们就都没问题了。

毅冰： 老实说，Fernando 先生，你真的让我有点为难。

Fernando 先生： 哎呀，这不难啦——只需要帮我们开拓市场。这就是我的请求！

毅冰： 我的老板会要我的命的！150 美元的操作费已经是我的底线了。真的不能再低了。

Fernando 先生： 这样吧，我可以把订单数量增加到 1200 件。但请保持 3.74 美元的单价，并且免除操作费。

毅冰： 稍等一下。我需要再确认一下。

Fernando 先生： 慢慢来。

毅冰： 我确认了一下，最低价格只能做到每件 3.82 美元。这真的已经是我的最终报价了。

Fernando 先生：哎呀，能不能把价格凑个整，3.80 美元怎么样？

毅冰：（笑）好吧，你赢了！3.80 美元，给我的贵宾客户！

Fernando 先生：非常感谢！这笔交易就这么定了。

Words & Phrases（词汇和句型）

circle back 返回

tough spot 困境

bump up 提升、提高

final number 最终价格（number 在这里，相当于 price）

You got me! 你打败我了！

Chinglish Correction（中式英语纠错）

我随后会下正式的订单。

【Chinglish】

I will place the formal order accordingly.

【Native English】

I will place the official order accordingly.

▶ 毅冰补充：

这句话不能通过字面意思去强行翻译，否则容易闹笑话。在英语中，一般没有 formal order 这个说法，而是用 official order 来表示"正式订单"。又比如说官方网站，是 official website。

27 拒绝无理要求，学高情商沟通技巧

故事背景 🖉

Fernando 先生想要新款太阳能灯的样品，但不仅要求在样品灯上体现他们公司的商标，还要按照他们设计好的彩盒完成包装，以便在欧洲跟分销商和零售商洽谈。但在毅冰看来，如果这样做的话，前期成本很大，要投入太多的费用，显然是不可能的。

Dialogue:

Yibing: So, I'll have my assistant arrange all the samples for you as soon as possible.

Mr. Fernando: Great, I'm looking forward to seeing them!

Yibing: Just a <u>heads-up</u>, we'll cover the cost of the samples, but we'll need you to take care of the freight charges.

Mr. Fernando: No problem at all. I'll provide you with my <u>courier account</u> details.

Yibing: Perfect.

Mr. Fernando: Oh, and don't forget to include my logo on all the samples and the packaging.

Yibing: Your logo? Hmm, that could be an issue. It takes time to create the <u>printing template</u>, and the cost for that isn't cheap.

Mr. Fernando: It's really important for me to have the logo on them when I show the samples to my clients.

Yibing: Would it be possible to go with <u>neutral packaging</u> for now?

Mr. Fernando: Absolutely not! We're one of the leading importers in

Italy, and we have our own branded items. I need to display these samples at our local trade fairs and use them in negotiations with distributors and retailers. Our brand image is crucial to how we present ourselves. We both want to win orders, right? So, let's work together on this.

Yibing: I get it. Let me check the cost of adding your logo and custom packaging, and I'll get back to you with the details.

Mr. Fernando: Yibing, this is part of your business expenses. You provide the samples for free, and I'll cover the shipping. That seems fair, doesn't it?

Yibing: I see your point. It is our responsibility to provide the samples at no charge. But you're asking for customized packaging, which incurs additional costs. It's only fair to share that extra expense.

Mr. Fernando: No way. None of my other suppliers have ever charged me for this.

Yibing: What if we agree to <u>refund</u> you the cost for the custom packaging once you place a full order? How does that sound?

Mr. Fernando: I'm only willing to cover the shipping costs—nothing more.

Yibing: I'm really sorry, but in that case, we won't be able to move forward with this.

参考译文 📖

毅冰：那，我会让我助理尽快为您安排所有样品。

Fernando 先生：太好了，我很期待看到这些样品！

毅冰：只想提前提醒一下，我们会承担样品的成本，但运费需要您来承担。

Fernando 先生：没问题，我会提供我的快递账户信息给你。

毅冰：完美。

Fernando 先生：哦，还有，别忘了把我的商标放在所有样品和包装上。

毅冰：您的商标？嗯，这可能会有点麻烦。制作印刷模板需要时间，而且成本也不便宜。

Fernando 先生：让商标出现在样品上对我来说非常重要，这样我可以展示给我的客户看。

毅冰：现在先用中性包装可以吗？

Fernando 先生：绝对不行！我们是意大利领先的进口商之一，而且我们有自己的品牌产品。我需要在当地的展会上展示这些样品，并在与分销商和零售商谈判时使用。我们的品牌形象对我们展示自己非常关键。我们都想拿到订单，对吧？所以让我们一起努力。

毅冰：我明白了。我会检查一下添加您商标和定制包装的成本，稍后给您回复。

Fernando 先生：毅冰，这应该算是你们的业务成本吧。你们提供免费样品，我来承担运费。这看起来很公平，不是吗？

毅冰：我明白您的意思。提供免费样品确实是我们的责任，但您要求定制包装，这会产生额外费用。共同分担这部分费用才是公平的。

Fernando 先生：绝对不行。我的其他供应商从来没有让我为此支付过费用。

毅冰：如果我们同意，在您下正式订单后退还您定制包装的费用呢？这个方案怎么样？

Fernando 先生：我只愿意承担运费，其他费用我不愿支付。

毅冰：非常抱歉，那我们可能无法继续推进了。

Words & Phrases（词汇和句型）

heads-up 事先提醒

courier account 快递账户

printing template 印刷模板

neutral packaging 中性包装（没有具体品牌信息的包装）

refund 退款

很抱歉，这已经是铁板钉钉的事情，没法改了。

【Chinglish】

Sorry. It was already confirmed, and couldn't be revised.

【Native English】

I'm sorry it cannot be revised. What done is done.

▶ **毅冰补充：**

形容"铁板钉钉"，表示已经确定的事情，在英文中可以用短语 what done is done 告诉对方"木已成舟""生米煮成熟饭"，尘埃落定，无法更改。

28 无法达成共识，随时切换替代方案

故事背景 ✎

对于 Fernando 先生的要求，毅冰无法接受，也不能承担过高的制版费，所以只能想办法找折中方案，从而促成交易。于是毅冰提出别的方案，双方各退一步，最终建议被 Fernando 采纳。

Dialogue:

Yibing: I understand you want to make a strong brand statement with these products, but I can assure you that the neutral packaging won't <u>diminish that impact</u>. We use high-quality, white <u>corrugated paper</u>, and we print with German-made Heidelberg presses for <u>top-tier</u> color quality.

Mr. Fernando: It's not just about the packaging or the solar lights. We're talking about the entire branding strategy here. Our clients need to trust our brand. OEM is fine, and ODM works too, but what really matters is that everything aligns with our product line and brand identity. That's non-negotiable.

Yibing: I completely understand where you're coming from.

Mr. Fernando: That's exactly why I'm insistent on this. It's not me being difficult, but protecting our brand's reputation is critical.

Yibing: You're definitely <u>easygoing</u>, but we're running into some challenges on this one.

Mr. Fernando: I'm listening—what's the issue?

Yibing: To create fully customized packaging with your logo will take extra time and add costs, especially for small sample quantities. However, I do have an alternative. We can use neutral packaging for the samples but include high-quality, custom-branded stickers with your logo and company information. This way, your clients will see the branding, but we avoid the delays and high costs of custom printing for such a <u>small batch</u>.

Mr. Fernando: And these stickers—are they included at no extra cost?

Yibing: Yes, absolutely. We'll handle the stickers at no additional charge.

Mr. Fernando: Okay, that sounds reasonable. But can you still meet my timeline? I need these samples ready and shipped out within 10 days. It's a bit tight.

Yibing: I'll be honest, that's a pretty tight deadline given the current production schedule, but I'll push the team to prioritize this. We'll do our best to meet that timeline.

Mr. Fernando: I appreciate that, but I need your commitment. This is crucial for an upcoming trade show, and any delay could impact our negotiations with distributors.

Yibing: I understand. I'll personally oversee this to make sure everything goes smoothly. If anything comes up that might affect the timeline, you'll be the first to know. But rest assured, I'll do everything I can to hit that 10-day window.

Mr. Fernando: That's what I like to hear—clear communication and proactive management. I'm counting on you, Yibing.

Yibing: You've got it. Let's move forward with this plan, and I'll get started right away.

Mr. Fernando: Great, we're on the same page now. Let's make this happen.

参考译文 📖

毅冰： 我理解您希望通过这些产品传递强烈的品牌形象，但我可以向您保证，中性包装不会削弱这一点。我们使用高质量的白色瓦楞纸，并且用德国制造的海德堡印刷机进行顶级的彩色印刷，效果非常出色。

Fernando 先生： 这里讨论的并不仅仅是包装或太阳能灯。这是整个品牌战略的问题。我们的客户需要信任我们的品牌。OEM 可以接受，ODM 也可以，但最重要的是所有东西都必须与我们的产品线和品牌形象保持一致。这是不能妥协的。

毅冰： 我完全理解您的想法。

Fernando 先生： 这就是为什么我如此坚持。这不是我在为难你，而是保护我们品牌的声誉至关重要。

毅冰： 您确实是个随和的人，但这次我们确实遇到了一些挑战。

Fernando 先生： 我听着，问题出在哪里？

毅冰： 为样品做完全定制的包装需要额外的时间和成本，尤其是对于少量样品。不过，我有一个替代方案。我们可以使用中性包装，但是为您提供带有您品牌标志和公司信息的高质量定制贴纸。这样，您的客户仍然可以看到品牌形象，而我们可以避免因小批量定制印刷导致的延误和高成本。

Fernando 先生：这些贴纸是免费的吗？

毅冰：是的，完全免费。我们不会收取额外费用。

Fernando 先生：好的，这听起来合理。但是你们还能按时完成吗？我需要这些样品在 10 天内准备好并寄出。时间有点紧张。

毅冰：说实话，考虑到当前的生产进度，这个时间相当紧，但我会推动团队优先处理这个项目。我们会尽最大努力满足这个时间要求。

Fernando 先生：我很感激，但我需要你的承诺。这对即将举行的展会非常关键，任何延误都会影响我们与分销商的谈判。

毅冰：我明白。我会亲自监督这个项目，确保一切顺利进行。如果有任何可能影响进度的问题，我会第一时间通知您。但请放心，我会尽全力确保在 10 天内完成。

Fernando 先生：这就是我想听到的——清晰的沟通和积极的管理。我相信你，毅冰。

毅冰：您放心吧。我们就按这个计划进行，我马上开始着手处理。

Fernando 先生：很好，现在我们达成一致了。让我们一起推动这件事。

Words & Phrases（词汇和句型）

diminish the impact 减少影响

corrugated paper 瓦楞纸

top-tier 顶尖的、顶级的（类似于 top-notch）

easygoing 好说话的、好相处的

small batch 小批量

Chinglish Correction（中式英语纠错）

我想在春节前拿下订单，纯粹是一厢情愿。

【Chinglish】

It is impossible to get the order before the CNY holiday.

【Native English】

I hope to get the order before the CNY holiday, but it is pure wishful thinking.

▶ **毅冰补充：**

"一厢情愿"这个词很难翻译，往往要根据语境，在理解上下文的语境下找到合适的用词。像 wishful thinking，就有"不太可能做到""非常为难"的意思，用在这里就相对妥当。而 impossible 的字眼则更加侧重于客观陈述。

---

29 样品出现问题，要有策略化险为夷

故事背景

> Fernando 先生回国不久，毅冰给他寄了样品。但是运气不太好，有几个产品在运输途中被损坏，Fernando 非常不高兴。毅冰连忙打电话过去道歉，表明立场，并立刻解决这个问题。

Dialogue:

Yibing: Hello, is Mr. Fernando available?

Mr. Fernando: Speaking. Who's calling?

Yibing: Mr. Fernando, it's Yibing from ABC Trading. How are you today?

Mr. Fernando: Honestly, not great. I'm pretty <u>frustrated</u> right now.

Yibing: I saw your email, and I want to sincerely apologize for the issues with the shipment. I completely understand how this has caused problems <u>on your end</u>.

Mr. Fernando: Frustrated isn't even the word. I had to show those damaged items to my clients, and it's <u>embarrassing</u>. This is damaging our relationship—and it's because of your company.

Yibing: I completely understand, and I'm really sorry for the inconvenience this has caused. This is definitely not the experience we want you or your clients to have.

Mr. Fernando: I need to know how you're going to fix this. My clients won't tolerate any more delays.

Yibing: Absolutely. I've already spoken to our team, and we're preparing new samples as we speak. I'll personally make sure they're shipped out early next week, and we'll cover the freight costs this time as it's our mistake. Once they're on the way, I'll send you the <u>tracking number</u> so you can follow up.

Mr. Fernando: That sounds better. But I'm really counting on you to get this right—no more <u>slip-ups</u>.

Yibing: I completely understand. I assure you this won't happen again. We'll make sure everything is handled perfectly this time.

Mr. Fernando: Alright, I'll hold you to that. Don't let me down again.

Yibing: You have my word, Mr. Fernando. I'll stay in touch with updates and make sure everything goes smoothly.

参考译文 📖

毅冰： 你好，请问 Fernando 先生在吗？

Fernando 先生： 我就是。你是哪位？

毅冰： Fernando 先生，我是 ABC 贸易公司的毅冰。您今天过得怎么样？

Fernando 先生： 说实话，不太好。我现在非常沮丧。

毅冰： 我看到了您的邮件，我真诚地为这次货物问题向您道歉。我完全理解这给您带来了很多麻烦。

Fernando 先生： 不仅仅是麻烦。我不得不把这些破损的产品展示给我的客户，真是太尴尬了。这已经影响到了我们的关系，而这一切都是因为你们公司的问题。

毅冰： 我完全理解您的感受，为此次带来的不便深感抱歉。这绝对不是我们希望您和您的客户经历的事情。

Fernando 先生： 我需要知道你们打算如何解决这个问题。我的客户已经无法容忍任何进一步的延误了。

毅冰： 您说得对。我已经和我们的团队沟通过了，我们正在准备新的样品。我会确保它们在下周初发出。由于我们的失误，这次我们会承担运费。货物发出后，我会把快递追踪号码发给您，方便您跟进。

Fernando 先生： 这样听起来好多了。但我真的希望你们这次能做好——不能再出错了。

毅冰： 我完全理解。我向您保证，这次绝对不会再出问题了。我们会确保一切顺利进行。

Fernando 先生： 好吧，我就等着看结果了。别再让我失望。

毅冰： 您尽管放心，Fernando 先生。我会随时关注最新情况，确保一切顺利进行。

Words & Phrases（词汇和句型）

frustrated 沮丧的、失落的

on your end 在你这边

embarrassing 令人尴尬的

tracking number 快递单号、快递追踪号码

slip-up 疏忽、错误、过失（相当于 mistake）

Chinglish Correction（**中式英语纠错**）

你决定吧！

【Chinglish】

You decide it!

【Native English】

Your call!

▶ **毅冰补充：**

　　这又是一句地道的口语表达，经常可以在好莱坞大片或美剧里听到这样的对话。如女主角问男主角，我们晚上去哪吃饭？对方回答"Your call!"，就是"你定吧""你做主吧"。

 30 项目深入探讨，关键对话推动进展

故事背景

　　时隔一个多月，Fernando 先生再次来到中国，跟毅冰约在公司见面。对于上次的样品，已经给他的客户们看过，综合了一些意见，所以过来跟毅冰进行下一轮的谈判。

Dialogue:

Yibing: Great to see you again, Mr. Fernando!

Mr. Fernando: Likewise. I can't help but notice things have changed quite a bit since I was last here.

Yibing: Yes, we've made some updates. We've added a few new products to the <u>lineup</u>. Would you like to take a quick look and see if anything grabs your attention?

Mr. Fernando: I'm excited to check them out, but before that, let's <u>get down to business</u>. The project we're working on takes priority right now.

Yibing: Absolutely, let's dive right in.

Mr. Fernando: So, first off, we're looking to scale back the initial order to 500 pieces. Given the current economic situation in Italy, we need to be cautious and test the waters before we go all in. I'm really trying to keep our budget in check and <u>minimize the risk</u>.

Yibing: I completely understand. What else is on your mind?

Mr. Fernando: The second point is the price—USD 3.80 per unit is just too high for us, especially since we're planning a seven-day promotional run with a <u>rock-bottom retail price</u>. We've set the retail price at EUR 4.99, so to make it work on our end, we need to be buying at no more than USD 2.50 per unit. I know that's a big ask, but that's why I'm here—to see if we can come up with a solution together.

Yibing: Mr. Fernando, I really appreciate you coming here and your trust in us. I understand where you're coming from, but to be honest, our manufacturing cost alone is above USD 2.50. To <u>hit your target price</u>, we'd need to make some adjustments. For example, we could switch from the Korean-made rechargeable batteries to Chinese-made ones, source more cost-effective stainless steel, or downgrade the packaging to a three-layer corrugated box. I'd need to run the numbers with our suppliers, but I can definitely explore these options and get back to you with a new price.

Mr. Fernando: Fair enough, that makes sense.

Yibing: As for the order quantity, we've talked about this before. We really can't do such a small quantity without adding a handling charge. One option would be to go with our own branding, which could help offset some of the costs, especially if we're promoting the products ourselves.

Mr. Fernando: I've already made it clear—no branding changes. We need to stick to our brand. That's a non-starter for us.

Yibing: I get it. Here's a thought—what if we meet halfway? We keep the packaging neutral—no branding—and then we add removable stickers with your brand and company info. That way, if the market doesn't respond the way you're hoping, you can send the unsold goods back to us. We can just remove the stickers and repurpose the products.

Mr. Fernando: Hmm, now you're talking. I think that could actually work for us.

Yibing: I'm glad to hear that. So, the only thing left on the table is the pricing. Let me circle back with our suppliers to finalize the cost, and I'll give you an update as soon as I have something concrete.

Mr. Fernando: Sounds good. Let's move forward with that and see what you come back with. I'm optimistic we can make this work.

Yibing: I'm confident we will. I'll keep you posted every step of the way.

参考译文

毅冰：很高兴再次见到您，Fernando 先生！

Fernando 先生：我也是。我注意到自从我上次来过之后，这里变化挺大的。

毅冰：是的，我们做了一些更新。我们在产品线中增加了一些新产品。您要不要稍微看看，看看有没有什么吸引您的款式？

Fernando 先生：我很期待看看这些新品，但首先，我们得先谈谈项

目。毕竟这是我现在优先处理的事情。

毅冰： 当然，咱们马上进入正题。

Fernando 先生： 首先，我们想把初次订单的数量减少到 500 件。考虑到意大利目前的经济状况，我们需要谨慎一些，先测试市场再说。我得严格控制预算，尽量降低风险。

毅冰： 我完全理解。还有什么其他的事情吗？

Fernando 先生： 第二点是价格——每件 3.80 美元对我们来说还是太高了，尤其是我们计划开展一个为期七天的促销活动，零售价定得非常低。我们已经将零售价定在 4.99 欧元，因此要想让我们这边有利润，我们需要每件的采购价控制在不超过 2.50 美元。我知道这要求有点高，但我来这里就是希望我们能一起找到解决方案。

毅冰： 我非常感谢您能来，也感谢您对我们的信任。我理解您的立场，但老实说，我们的制造成本已经超过 2.50 美元。要达到您的目标价格，我们需要做一些调整。比如说，我们可以把韩国制造的充电电池换成中国制造的，选择更经济的 304 不锈钢，或者将彩盒包装降级为三层瓦楞纸包装。我需要和我们的供应商核算这些调整的费用，但我可以探索这些选项，并尽快给您一个新的报价。

Fernando 先生： 这很公平，有道理。

毅冰： 至于订单数量的问题，我们之前已经讨论过了。如果订单量这么小，我们真的无法免除操作费。一种选择是使用我们的品牌，这样可以帮助分摊一些成本，尤其是如果我们自己推广这些产品的话。

Fernando 先生： 我之前已经明确过了——不能改变品牌。我们必须坚持用我们的品牌，这是没得谈的。

毅冰： 我明白。那我有个想法——我们折中一下如何？我们保持中性包装，不加品牌，然后贴上带您品牌和公司信息的可移除贴纸。这样，如果市场反应不佳，您可以将未售出的商品退还给我们，我们撕掉贴纸，再重新利用这些产品。

Fernando 先生：嗯，这样说就对了。我觉得这个方案可行。

毅冰：听到您这么说我很高兴。那么现在只剩下价格的问题了。我会和我们的供应商联系，确认最终的成本，一有消息我会尽快给您。

Fernando 先生：听起来不错。我们就按这个方案继续推进，看看你那边能提供什么。我对达成协议还是抱有希望的。

毅冰：我相信我们能解决这个问题。我会随时向您汇报进展的。

Words & Phrases（词汇和句型）

lineup 阵容（这里指的是产品系列）

get down to business 言归正传、开始谈正事

minimize the risk 把风险降到最低

rock-bottom retail price 最低零售价

hit your target price 达到你的目标价格

Chinglish Correction（中式英语纠错）

晕！我忘记给你发报价单了！

【Chinglish】

Sorry, I forgot to send you the offer sheet.

【Native English】

Shoot! I forgot to send you the offer sheet.

▶ **毅冰补充：**

这句的核心，是怎么合适表达这个"晕"，既能切合语境，又能让对方明白。在美剧《老友记》里，女主角 Rachel 就非常喜欢用 Shoot 这个词作为口头禅，意思就是"晕倒""真倒霉""哦，天哪"。很多时候，跟"My god!"的用法相近。前一句的表达当然没有错误，只是第二句用了 Shoot，更加口语化。

谈判高阶技能，
这些地道表达
你真的会吗

31 价格谈判，业务人员的必经之路

故事背景

美国客户 Amy 是当地连锁超市的买手，有兴趣从毅冰公司采购一款工作灯。预期订单数量非常可观，但是价格是横亘在两人之间的大问题。双方拉锯，逐步展开谈判。

Dialogue:

Amy: Have you supplied this product to any US retailers yet?

Yibing: Which one? The 35 LEDs work light?

Amy: Yes, the KJ-1039 model.

Yibing: Not yet. We've primarily been distributing it to Germany and the Benelux region.

Amy: The color combination really stands out.

Yibing: Thank you!

Amy: Is it shockproof?

Yibing: Yes, it is.

Amy: Waterproof as well?

Yibing: You bet! It's both shockproof and waterproof.

Amy: Good. What kind of pricing are we talking about?

Yibing: That depends on your order quantity. Could you share the volume you're considering?

Amy: What's your MOQ, and what's the unit price at that quantity?

Yibing: Our usual price is USD 26.80 per piece, with color box packaging, and the MOQ is 1000 pieces.

Amy: How many can fit into a 40-foot container?

Yibing: Roughly 2200 pieces.

Amy: And in a 40-foot high cube?

Yibing: About 2900 pieces.

Amy: I'm looking at 5800 pieces—two 40-foot high cubes. What's your best price at that quantity?

Yibing: For that volume, we can reduce the price by USD 2, bringing it down to USD 24.80 per unit.

Amy: Yibing, keep in mind this is just a trial order. We have over 300 stores across the US, so this is a big opportunity for you to break into the US market. We're looking to build a long-term partnership here, not just one order.

Yibing: You're absolutely right, Amy. That's exactly what we're aiming for as well—a lasting business relationship.

Amy: Here's what I need. I'd like a 25% discount.

Yibing: I'm sorry, but a 25% reduction just isn't feasible at this point.

Amy: Oh, I think it's very possible. If you can meet my target of USD 20 per unit, I'll place the order right now. If not, I'll have to move forward with another supplier. Come on, Yibing, give me your BEST offer.

参考译文 📖

Amy：你们有把这款产品供应给美国的零售商吗？

毅冰：您指的是这款 35 个 LED 的工作灯吗？

Amy：对，KJ-1039 型号。

毅冰：还没有。我们主要将这款产品销往德国和比荷卢地区。

Amy：这款颜色搭配很抢眼。

毅冰：谢谢！

Amy：它是防震的吗？

毅冰：是的，防震。

Amy：防水呢？

毅冰：你说对了！当然，它既防震又防水。

Amy：很好。那么价格是多少？

毅冰：这取决于您的采购数量。您能告知一下您预期的订单量吗？

Amy：你们的最小起订量是多少？在这个数量下，单价是多少？

毅冰：我们的通常价格是每件 26.80 美元，彩盒包装，最小起订量是 1000 件。

Amy：一个 40 英尺的集装箱可以装多少件？

毅冰：大约 2200 件。

Amy：那 40 尺高柜呢？

毅冰：大约 2900 件。

Amy：我打算订 5800 件，也就是两个 40 尺高柜。在这个数量下，你能给到我什么价格？

毅冰：对于这个数量，我们可以降价 2 美元，每件 24.80 美元。

Amy：毅冰，记住，这只是一个试订单。我们在美国有超过 300 家门店，这对你们进入美国市场来说是个非常好的机会。我们希望建立的是长期的合作关系，而不仅仅是一笔订单。

毅冰：您说得对，Amy。这也是我们所追求的——长期的业务合作。

Amy：我需要的是 25% 的折扣。

毅冰：抱歉，目前这个折扣幅度我们做不到。

Amy：我觉得这是完全可以的。如果你能达到我每件 20 美元的目标价，我现在就下单。如果不行，我可能得找其他供应商。毅冰，给我你最好的报价吧。

Words & Phrases（词汇和句型）

Benelux region 比荷卢地区（比利时、荷兰、卢森堡三个国家的简写）

stand out 脱颖而出、夺人眼球

You bet! 你说对了！

shockproof and waterproof 防震和防水

40-foot high cube 40 尺高柜

Chinglish Correction（中式英语纠错）

如果给你 25% 的折扣，我们会损失很大的。

【Chinglish】

If we give you the 25% discount, we will lose a lot!

【Native English】

We will break the bank if we give you the discount of 25%.

▶ 毅冰补充：

这里用了一个短语，"break the bank"，表示"损失很大""亏大了""大出血"等，比直接翻译要更加灵活和口语化。

32　数量谈判，方法技巧的精细运用

故事背景 ✏️

　　Amy 显然是专业买手，砍价非常狠。毅冰一边退让，一边在试探 Amy 的底线。所谓的目标价，明显是 Amy 打出的一张试探牌，为进一步砍价做铺垫。毅冰不慌不忙，先通过数量的问题"兜圈子"，再慢慢寻找切入点，从而让谈判继续进行。

Dialogue:

Yibing: Alright, you got me! The price we offered to our Belgian client was USD 25.10 per piece, and that's as true as it gets.

Amy: That's irrelevant to me. The US market is different—you need to be far more competitive here. You'll have to rethink your <u>profit margins</u>.

Yibing: You're absolutely right. We really need your partnership to help us <u>break into the US market.</u>

Amy: Exactly. This has to be a collaborative effort if it's going to work.

Yibing: Let me talk to my boss, and I'll push for the best possible price for you.

Amy: I'll expect a better offer soon.

Yibing: Also, while we're on it, if you can increase your order to 10000 pieces, I'm confident we can give you an even better discount.

Amy: Yibing, the quantity isn't the issue right now. It's all about the price.

Yibing: I understand, but pricing fluctuates with order volume. The more you order, the better the deal I can give you.

Amy: My <u>cap</u> is 5800 pieces, no more. I can't justify placing a larger order until we see how the market reacts. Right now, I'm taking a big gamble on this product. It's new, and we have no idea how US consumers will respond. So, don't disappoint me.

Yibing: I hear you. I've got all the details down. Please give me a day or two to go over everything with my team, and I'll send you the <u>revised offer</u> in writing.

Amy: Good. I'm looking for something solid when you come back to me. Time is money, Yibing. I need to be able to present this to my team as a <u>competitive option</u>, or I'll have to move on to other suppliers.

Yibing: I understand, Amy. I'll make sure the next offer meets your expectations. We value this opportunity, and I'll do everything I can to make sure you're happy with the final price.

Amy: You should. I'm giving you access to over 300 stores, a huge platform for your product. But it has to make financial sense on my end, too. If we can get the right price, this could be the start of a strong partnership.

Yibing: I agree. I'll make sure you get the numbers you need to make this a success for both of us.

参考译文 📖

毅冰： 好吧，你说服我了！之前我们给比利时客户的报价是每件 25.10 美元，这是千真万确的。

Amy： 这和我没关系。美国市场不同——在这里你们需要更具竞争力。你得重新考虑你的利润空间。

毅冰： 您说得完全正确。我们确实需要您的合作来帮助我们打入美国市场。

Amy： 没错。如果要成功，这必须是双方的合作努力。

毅冰：我需要和我的老板讨论一下，我会尽力给您争取最好的价格。

Amy：我期待你尽快给出更好的报价。

毅冰：顺便提一下，如果您能将订单增加到 10000 件，我相信我们可以给您更大的折扣。

Amy：毅冰，现在不是数量的问题，而是价格。

毅冰：我理解，但价格确实会随着订单数量的增加而发生变化。订单越大，价格就越优惠。

Amy：5800 件是我的上限，不能再多了。在看到市场反应之前，我不能下更大的订单。现在，我对这款产品的销售是下一场巨大的赌注。这是新产品，没人知道美国消费者的反应会如何。所以，别让我失望。

毅冰：我听明白了。我已经记下所有细节。请给我一两天时间，我会和我的团队讨论，然后通过邮件发给您修改后的报价。

Amy：好的。我期待你给我一个实在的报价。时间就是金钱，毅冰。我需要能够向我的团队呈现一个有竞争力的选项，否则我就得考虑其他供应商了。

毅冰：我明白，Amy。我会确保下一个报价符合您的期望。我们非常重视这个机会，我会尽一切努力让您对最终价格感到满意。

Amy：你应该这样做。我为你提供了进入 300 多家门店的机会，这是一个巨大的平台来推广你们的产品。但这对我来说也必须要有经济上的收益。如果我们能达成合适的价格，这将会是我们建立强大合作关系的开始。

毅冰：我同意。我会确保您得到您需要的报价，让这次合作对我们双方来说都是成功的。

Words & Phrases（词汇和句型）

profit margin 利润率

break into the US market 打入美国市场

cap 最高限额（在这里，指的是最大数量）

revised offer 修改后的报价

competitive option 有竞争力的选择

Chinglish Correction（中式英语纠错）

我们希望能接到正式订单，收回我们前期投入的模具成本。

【Chinglish】

We hope to get the official order to refund the tooling charge.

【Native English】

We hope to get the official order soon, to recoup the previous investment of tooling cost.

▶ **毅冰补充：**

在英语中，"收回"可以用 recoup 这个动词，"收回成本"是 recoup the cost，"收回投资"是 recoup the investment；而 refund 更侧重于退回，如 tax refund，就是我们常说的"退税"。

---

33 索赔谈判，要从困境中获得突破

故事背景

老客户 Ron 跟毅冰在公司里碰面，Ron 向毅冰抱怨供货的工作灯存在质量问题。LED 灯经常会出现不亮的情况，有很多消费者退货，造成很大的库存压力，所以不得不向毅冰索赔，并讨论后续的合作问题。

Dialogue:

Ron: So, what's the plan here, Yibing? Can you give me a solution today?

Yibing: I'm truly sorry, Ron. We're fully committed to resolving this issue. When we received your first complaint, we held an internal meeting and conducted several rounds of testing. As more evidence came in, our engineering team discovered that the LED <u>lifespan</u> wasn't meeting our standards.

Ron: So, it's the LED that's faulty—not the PCB board or the overall structure?

Yibing: Correct. We've shipped three batches of this work light to you, and I can confirm that the problem only occurred with the first batch. We switched LED manufacturers after that and started sourcing them from Korea for the second and third waves.

Ron: Well, I've had multiple consumer complaints, and we've seen a significant number of returns.

Yibing: I understand the frustration. If you're planning a <u>recall</u>, it should only affect the first batch of items.

Ron: And how are consumers supposed to tell which batch they have?

Yibing: No need to worry. I'll provide you with the article numbers, and consumers will be able to identify them easily by checking the packaging.

Ron: Alright. But let's talk compensation. You need to refund me for the first order, and that includes not just the cost of the goods but also my lost margin, sea freight charges, import duties, inland transport, express shipping, and more.

Yibing: I see.

Ron: <u>To put it bluntly,</u> you're looking at about three times the original order cost in compensation.

Yibing: That's... quite a hit. You're killing me here!

Ron: I'm just being honest, Yibing. We're both in this business to make money, and this situation has put me in a <u>tough spot</u>. I'm holding a lot of unsellable inventory.

Yibing: I get it, Ron, I really do. Would it be possible for us to refund the payment for the first order and then spread the rest of the compensation over future orders? Maybe we could deduct $1000 from each order until the full amount is settled.

Ron: That's not going to work for me.

Yibing: What if, instead, we compensate you with a new batch of products at no charge? That way, you can keep your inventory flowing, and we'll still cover the value of the faulty goods.

Ron: I'm not thrilled about that idea either. The last thing I need is more stock sitting in my warehouse that I can't sell if something goes wrong again. I need this to be sorted in a way that doesn't leave me holding the bag.

Yibing: I completely understand. What if we send over a new wave of goods with a different product line as compensation, something that's proven to sell well? We'll cover the cost, and you'll have something fresh to offer your customers. We want to make this right and rebuild the trust here.

Ron: Now you're getting closer to something reasonable. But I'll need assurances on the quality this time—no more slip-ups, Yibing. I can't afford another round of returns.

Yibing: Absolutely. We'll ensure rigorous quality control on everything moving forward. I'll personally oversee the process and keep you updated every step of the way.

Ron: Good. I need to feel confident in this. If we can <u>get this sorted</u>, I'm willing to keep the partnership going, but I need to see results.

Yibing: You have my word, Ron. We value this relationship, and I'll make sure we turn things around.

参考译文 📖

Ron：所以，毅冰，你有什么计划？今天能给我一个解决方案吗？

毅冰：我真的很抱歉，Ron。我们全力以赴解决这个问题。当我们收到您的第一个投诉时，就立即召开了内部会议，并进行了几轮测试。随着更多证据的出现，我们的工程团队发现 LED 的使用寿命没有达到我们的标准。

Ron：所以问题是出在 LED，而不是 PCB 板或整体结构？

毅冰：没错。我们给您发了三批这种工作灯，我可以确认问题只出现在第一批。我们在那之后更换了 LED 供应商，并在第二批和第三批产品中使用了从韩国进口的 LED。

Ron：好吧，我们收到了很多消费者的投诉，也有不少退货。

毅冰：我理解您的沮丧。如果您打算召回，请只针对第一批次的产品。

Ron：那消费者怎么区分他们拿到的是哪一批次呢？

毅冰：不用担心。我会给您提供产品编号，消费者可以通过包装上的信息轻松识别。

Ron：好吧。现在我们得谈谈赔偿问题。你需要退还我第一批订单的货款，还要赔偿我的利润损失、海运费、进口税、内陆运输费用、快递费用等。

毅冰：我明白了。

Ron：说得直白点，这大概是原订单成本的三倍赔偿。

毅冰：这……可真是个大打击。你干脆"杀"了我算了！

Ron：我只是实话实说，毅冰。我们都是做生意的，而这次的情况让我陷入了一个艰难的境地。现在我有一堆卖不出去的库存。

毅冰：我理解，Ron，我真的理解。那我们能不能先退还第一批订单的货款，剩下的赔偿分摊到未来的订单中呢？也许我们可以每次从订单里扣掉 1000 美元，直到赔偿完。

Ron：这对我来说行不通。

毅冰：那如果我们免费提供一批新产品作为赔偿呢？这样您可以保持库存流动，我们也能补偿掉有问题的那部分货值。

Ron：我也不太喜欢这个想法。我最不需要的就是仓库里堆满了卖不出去的货物，如果再出问题，我可不想再承受一次。我需要一个不会让我"背锅"的解决方案。

毅冰：我完全理解。如果我们用另一种畅销的产品线的新品作为补偿呢？我们会承担成本，这样您也有新产品提供给客户。我们真的想解决问题，并重建信任。

Ron：现在你说了一个比较合理的方案了。不过我需要保证这次的产品质量，不能再有问题了，毅冰。我不能再承受一次退货了。

毅冰：当然。这次我们会加强所有的质量控制。我会亲自监督整个过程，并及时向您汇报进展。

Ron：好。我需要对这个方案有信心。如果我们能妥善解决这个问题，我愿意继续合作，但我要看到结果。

毅冰：您可以相信我，Ron。我们非常重视这段合作关系，我会确保这次问题得到彻底解决。

Words & Phrases（词汇和句型）

lifespan 使用寿命

recall 召回（一般产品出现重大问题，往往需要 recall，就是全面召回）

to put it bluntly 不客气地说、直截了当地说

tough spot 艰难的境地

get this sorted 解决这个问题

Chinglish Correction（中式英语纠错）

抱歉回复晚了，我电脑昨天出了点问题。

【Chinglish】

Sorry for late reply, because my computer was broken yesterday.

【Native English】

Sorry for late reply, as my computer froze up yesterday.

▶ **毅冰补充：**

描述"电脑出了点问题"，常用的短语是 freeze up。它表示电脑有点儿问题故障，电脑死机了，或者软件有一些毛病，又或者连不上网络等。而 be broken 则比较严重，一般用于形容电脑整个损坏，或者从外部遭到破坏。

34 品质谈判，用专业展示解决疑虑

故事背景

展会结束后，一个美国进口商 Raymond 前来拜访。他谈及一款充电的、用在户外雨伞上的伞灯，想让毅冰开发。因为是全新的产品，涉及品质、工艺、模具，以及生产过程中可能会遇到的方方面面的问题，需要深入探讨。

Dialogue:

Raymond: So, here's the initial <u>construction drawing</u>. You can make revisions based on the actual production requirements.

Yibing: Got it. The design looks fantastic!

Raymond: Thanks! We have a young and energetic team working on product development. They're full of <u>creative ideas</u>.

Yibing: Not just creative—this design is truly impressive.

Raymond: You're too kind!

Yibing: I actually discussed this with my boss and our chief engineer this morning, and we all agreed that adding a 4-function switch would be ideal for this product. It would allow the options of "2 lights on" "4 lights on" "4 lights flashing" and "off".

Raymond: So you're suggesting just adding the "2 lights on" option, right?

Yibing: Exactly. Think about it—when couples are enjoying a <u>candlelit dinner</u> under the garden umbrella, a softer, dimmer light would be perfect. It's not just about saving energy, it's about setting the right mood.

Raymond: (laughing...) That's great! And when they don't need any light at all, just turn it off. Simple and effective.

Yibing: (laughing...) Exactly, you get it! But seriously, for the body of the lamp, we'd suggest using propylene polymer. It's safe, eco-friendly, and contains no heavy metals.

Raymond: That sounds good to me.

Yibing: Now, when it comes to the LEDs, we have two options. We can either source them locally from China or import them from the US. Of course, the pricing will vary. What's your preference?

Raymond: Let's look at both options. Send me the pricing for each, and I'll review it.

Yibing: Will do. Now, there's one more thing—the <u>tooling cost</u>. It's going to be quite high, around USD 45000 for the molds and setup.

Raymond: Wow, that's steep. Can your company cover those costs?

Yibing: Unfortunately, we can't cover the full cost, but we're willing to share 20% as a <u>gesture of goodwill</u>. Additionally, if your orders reach 50000 units, we'll refund 30% of the tooling cost. And when the total order volume hits 150000 units, we'll refund the remaining 50%. I believe this is a fair arrangement for both sides to get started.

Raymond: That's something I'll have to consider. Please send me a detailed breakdown with all the pricing, descriptions, packaging details, tooling costs—basically, everything. You understand what I'm asking for, right?

Yibing: Absolutely. I'll make sure you have everything crystal clear.

参考译文 📖

Raymond：这是初步的结构图，你可以根据实际的生产需求进行修改。

毅冰：明白了。设计非常棒！

Raymond：谢谢！我们有一个年轻且充满活力的团队负责产品开发。他们很有创意。

毅冰：不仅是创意，设计真的很出彩。

Raymond：你太客气了！

毅冰：今天早上我已经和我的老板以及首席工程师讨论过了，我们一致认为，给这个产品增加一个四功能开关是理想的选择。它可以提供"2灯亮""4灯亮""4灯闪烁""关闭"这四种模式。

Raymond：你是说建议增加"2灯亮"的功能，对吧？

毅冰：没错。想象一下，当情侣在花园伞下享受烛光晚餐时，柔和的、较暗的灯光更合适。这不仅仅是节能，还能营造更好的氛围。

Raymond：（笑）这太棒了！而且如果不需要任何灯光，只要关掉就行了。简单又有效。

毅冰：（笑）完全正确！不过说真的，关于灯体，我们建议使用丙烯聚合物。这种材料安全、环保，并且不含重金属。

Raymond：听起来不错。

毅冰：至于 LED，我们有两个选择。可以在中国本地采购，也可以从美国进口。当然，价格会有所不同。您更倾向于哪种方案呢？

Raymond：两种方案都发给我吧。分别报个价，我会审核的。

毅冰：好的。还有一个问题就是模具成本。这部分费用会比较高，大约需要 4.5 万美元。

Raymond：哇，这价格有点高。你们公司能承担这些费用吗？

毅冰：很抱歉，我们无法全额承担，但我们愿意承担 20% 的费用，以示我们的诚意。另外，如果订单量达到 5 万件，我们将退还 30% 的模具费用。订单累计达到 15 万件时，我们会退还剩下的 50%。我认为这是一个对双方都公平的合作起点。

Raymond：我得考虑一下。请发给我一份详细的清单，包括所有的价格、描述、包装细节、模具费用等所有内容。你明白我的意思，对吧？

毅冰：完全明白。我会确保所有信息都非常清晰。

Words & Phrases（词汇和句型）

construction drawing 结构图纸

creative idea 创造性的想法、创意

candlelit dinner 烛光晚餐

tooling cost 模具费

gesture of goodwill 善意的姿态、友好的态度

Chinglish Correction（中式英语纠错）

你猜对了！

【Chinglish】

Your guess is right!

【Native English】

You betcha!

▶ **毅冰补充：**

猜对、猜测、猜想，不要总是用中文生硬地去翻译，不一定非要使用 guess 这个词。在口语里有一个句型"You betcha!"就表示"You're right!"或"You're correct!"的含义，也完全契合语境。

35 | 交货谈判，推动实现双赢

故事背景

> Raymond 的第一个订单已经确认，但是眼前最大的问题就是交货期。因为要开模具、打样、测试，还有各种不稳定因素，所以交货期无法加快，Raymond 非常焦急。

Dialogue:

Raymond: Yibing, I can't wait 90 days. We need these shipped sooner.

Yibing: Trust me, I completely understand, Raymond. I wish we could speed things up too. To be honest, the actual production time is only about 20 days. But since this is a brand-new product, we still need to build the molds, do the sampling, conduct factory audits, inspections, and supervise the loading. All of these steps take up quite a bit of time. By the way, do you want <u>third-party testing</u> for this order?

Raymond: Yes, we'll need to test for ETL certification.

Yibing: Oh no... Well, in that case, the timeline just got even longer. We're looking at 105 days now because we'll need to set aside at least two weeks for the testing phase.

Raymond: Yibing, that's way too late! Shipping alone takes at least 20 days to reach the US port, and I'll need another 5 to 10 days for inland delivery and distribution. There's no way I'll be able to make it in time for the <u>Christmas promotions</u>.

Yibing: I understand. What if we <u>split the shipment</u>? We can air freight around 20% of the order so you'll have enough stock to start promoting early. The rest of the shipment can come by sea and arrive after the holidays.

Raymond: That could work. If we can get the initial batch in before the holiday season, I could still retail them in time for Valentine's Day.

Yibing: Perfect! That gives you enough flexibility to keep things moving.

参考译文 📖

Raymond：毅冰，我等不了 90 天。我们需要更早发货。

毅冰： 我完全理解，Raymond。我也希望我们能加快进度。老实说，实际的生产时间只有大约 20 天。但因为这是一个全新的产品，我们还需要进行模具制作、样品测试、工厂审核、检查以及装货监督。所有这些步骤都非常耗时。顺便问一下，您这批订单需要第三方测试吗？

Raymond：是的，我们需要进行 ETL 认证检测。

毅冰： 哦，天哪……那样的话，时间线就更长了。现在看起来我们需要 105 天，因为检测阶段至少需要两周的时间。

Raymond：毅冰，这实在太晚了！光是运到美国港口就需要至少 20

天，我还需要再花 5 到 10 天进行内陆运输和分销。这样我根本赶不上圣诞促销季了。

毅冰：我明白。那我们分批发货怎么样？我们可以空运大约 20% 的订单，这样您就可以提前开始促销。剩下的货物可以走海运，在节日后到达。

Raymond：这样或许可以。如果我们能在节日前收到首批货物，我还可以赶上情人节的销售季。

毅冰：太好了！这样您就能灵活推进进度了。

Words & Phrases（词汇和句型）

speed things up 加快事情进展

factory audit 验厂（也经常表达成 factory evaluation）

third-party testing 第三方检测

Christmas promotions 圣诞促销季

split the shipment 分批出运

Chinglish Correction（中式英语纠错）

我们会在收到货 30 天内付款。

【Chinglish】

We will settle the payment 30 days after we receive the goods.

【Native English】

The payment will be settled 30 days net.

▶ 毅冰补充：

在口语中，或者使用电子邮件时，可以用 30 days net 表示"收货后 30 天"。在平时的聊天工具或者邮件书写中，也可简化成 Net 30，对方往往能看明白。

36 标准谈判，测试要求的精准处理

故事背景 ✐

> 　　Raymond 确认了订单交货期，但是比较担心能否通过检测认证，从而顺利推进整个项目。毅冰告知对方无须整个灯做 ETL 认证，只要电源适配器通过认证就可以。而 FCC 认证和 Energy Star 的认证，也没有问题。

Dialogue:

Yibing: Raymond, please don't worry. We'll be purchasing an ETL-approved power adaptor, so you're covered there.

Raymond: But aren't you going to apply for the ETL certification for the entire product set?

Yibing: It's not necessary, my friend. Since this is a lithium battery-powered device using DC power, not AC. US regulations only require the ETL certification for the adaptor. The rest of the product is exempt from that specific certification.

Raymond: Got it. What about the FCC testing? Where do we stand with that?

Yibing: That's not an issue at all. We've already got the FCC certification, and it's been issued by a third-party lab.

Raymond: Was it done by BV?

Yibing: No, it was done through Intertek.

Raymond: Ah, Intertek. That's great! So with the certifications in place, can you ship the goods earlier? It sounds like most of the hurdles have been cleared, and there shouldn't be any more delays.

Yibing: Not entirely, Raymond. While the FCC and ETL certifications are good to go, we're still in the process of preparing samples for the Energy Star testing.

Raymond: Is Energy Star certification really necessary for the US market?

Yibing: It's not mandatory right now, but we believe it's a strong selling point. Consumers trust the Energy Star label—it's like the GS certification in Germany. It's not required by law, but it's influential enough to drive purchasing decisions. Having it on the product will give us an edge and encourage impulse buys for a lot of customers.

Raymond: That makes sense. It's all about building consumer confidence. You really know your stuff!

Yibing: Thanks, Raymond. We want to make sure all bases are covered, so you can rest assured that we'll take care of everything.

参考译文 📖

毅冰：Raymond，请不必担心。我们会采购通过 ETL 认证的电源适配器，所以这方面已经没问题了。

Raymond：但你们不为整个产品申请 ETL 认证吗？

毅冰：不需要，朋友。因为这是一个使用直流电的锂电池设备，而不是交流电。根据美国的规定，只需要为电源适配器提供 ETL 认证。产品的其他部分不需要这个认证。

Raymond：明白了。那 FCC 测试怎么样？我们现在进展到哪一步了？

毅冰：这完全不是问题。我们已经拿到了 FCC 认证，由第三方实验室出具的。

Raymond：是 BV 做的吗？

毅冰：不是，是 Intertek 做的。

Raymond：啊，Intertek。那太好了！既然认证都已经到位，那可以早点发货了吗？听起来大部分障碍已经清除了，应该不会再延迟了吧。

毅冰：不完全是，Raymond。虽然 FCC 和 ETL 认证已经完成，但我们还在准备样品用于 Energy Star 的测试。

Raymond：Energy Star 认证对于美国市场真的有必要吗？

毅冰：目前不是强制性的，但我们认为它是一个非常强的卖点。消费者非常信任 Energy Star 标识——就像德国的 GS 认证一样。虽然法律上不强制要求，但它足够有影响力，可以推动购买决策。产品上有这个标识将会给我们带来竞争优势，并吸引很多消费者冲动购买。

Raymond：这很有道理。一切都是为了建立消费者的信心。你真是行家啊！

毅冰：谢谢，Raymond。我们会确保所有事情都处理好，您可以放心。

Words & Phrases（词汇和句型）

power adaptor 电源适配器

DC power 直流电（相对应交流电是 AC power）

third-party lab 第三方实验室

BV 法国国际检验局（非常知名的第三方测试机构 Bureau Veritas）

hurdle 障碍、难关、阻碍

Chinglish Correction（中式英语纠错）

到了那里你就随机应变吧。

【Chinglish】

Please do it by yourself when you arrive there.

【Native English】

You could try to play to the score tactically when you arrive there.

▶ **毅冰补充：**

这句话的翻译，本身就应当灵活调整，要尽量避免直译。do it by yourself 仅仅只是自己解决的意思，缺少"随机应变"的意味，英语中 play to the score tactically 更能表达这层意思。

37 付款谈判，决定核心利益的对话

故事背景

老客户 Vincent 来中国出差，再次拜访毅冰。他选了几款新产品下确认订单，也谈了几个老产品的返单。合作久了，Vincent 提出要修改原有的付款方式，毅冰一边让步，一边尽力谈判。

Dialogue:

Yibing: So, that's a total of five orders—two <u>repeat orders</u> for the PT-9984 model, and three new orders for the solar light, camping light, and work light. Thank you so much, Vincent!

Vincent: I hope this brightens your day a little.

Yibing: It certainly does! Much appreciated.

Vincent: No problem. So, what about the item numbers?

Yibing: My assistant is entering them into the system right now. Since these are new items, it'll take just a moment. Once they're in, I'll get the exact numbers for you.

Vincent: Got it.

Yibing: After that, I'll prepare and print the PIs for you. It would be great if you could sign them today.

Vincent: Sure, but as I mentioned before, we need to revisit the payment terms. Going forward, I'd like to <u>switch</u> to O/A 30 days. It's a standard practice we offer to our key suppliers.

Yibing: Vincent, I completely understand your position, but it's tough for us. We usually only accept T/T with a deposit or <u>L/C at sight—no exceptions so far.</u>

Vincent: I get that, but I'm placing larger and larger orders with you. The deposit is starting to add up, and honestly, it's creating some <u>cash flow challenges</u> on my end. I'm paying you 30% upfront, but on my side, I'm working with O/A 60 days with my own customers.

Yibing: I hear you, Vincent. I really value our long-term relationship, and I want to help you grow your market. I've brought this up with my boss several times to see how we can make this work.

Vincent: So, what can you offer?

Yibing: To keep our business growing together, we're willing to lower the deposit to 10%. The remaining 90% can be paid within two weeks of receiving the Bill of Lading.

Vincent: No chance we could move to full O/A terms with no deposit at all?

Yibing: Vincent, I'm always honest with you. Right now, we need a bit of a transition period. Let's start with this arrangement, and I believe we can revisit the deposit terms and maybe reduce it further before the end of the year.

Vincent: Alright, work your magic then.

Yibing: You know I will, Vincent. It's my job to make sure we both succeed.

参考译文 📖

毅冰： 所以，总共是五个订单——两个是 PT-9984 型号的返单，另外三个是太阳能灯、露营灯和工作灯的新订单。非常感谢您，Vincent！

Vincent： 希望这能让你今天开心一点。

毅冰： 当然！非常感谢。

Vincent： 没问题。那么，产品编号呢？

毅冰： 我的助理正在把它们录入系统。因为这些是新产品，需要一点时间。等录入完毕后，我会把准确的编号给您。

Vincent： 明白了。

毅冰： 之后我会准备并打印形式发票。如果今天您能签字，那就再好不过了。

Vincent： 当然，但正如我之前提到的，我们需要重新讨论一下付款方式。接下来，我希望改成 30 天账期。这是我们给核心供应商的标准做法。

毅冰： Vincent，我完全理解您的立场，但对我们来说这很难。我们通常只接受电汇加定金或即期信用证，目前没有例外。

Vincent： 我明白，但我现在给你的订单越来越大，预付款的金额也越来越高。坦白说，这对我的现金流造成了一定压力。我付给你 30% 的预付款，而我这边是给客户提供 60 天的账期。

毅冰： 我理解您的情况，Vincent。我非常重视我们长期的合作关系，也希望能够帮助您扩展市场。我已经和我的老板多次讨论，看我们能不能找到一个解决方案。

Vincent： 那你们能提供什么方案呢？

毅冰： 为了让我们能继续合作并共同发展，我们愿意将预付款降到 10%，剩下的 90% 可以在收到提单两周内支付。

Vincent： 那有没有可能完全采用账期，不需要预付款呢？

毅冰： Vincent，您知道我一直都对您很坦诚。现在我们需要一点儿过渡时间。我们先从这个方案开始，我相信在年底前，我们可以重新讨论预付款的比例，或许可以再降低一些。

Vincent：好吧，那就看你的了。

毅冰：您知道我会尽力的，Vincent。这就是我的工作，确保我们双方都成功。

Words & Phrases（词汇和句型）

repeat order 返单

switch 切换

L/C at sight 即期信用证

no exceptions so far 迄今为止没有例外

cash flow challenges 现金流的压力

Chinglish Correction（中式英语纠错）

我们希望本周内收到定金，请抓紧时间安排。

【Chinglish】

We hope to receive the deposit within this week. Please hurry up to arrange it.

【Native English】

Please cut it close and let us receive the deposit within this week.

▶ **毅冰补充：**

在口语中，"抓紧时间"可以使用固定短语 cut it close，常用的 hurry up 只是让对方尽快，与要表达的"抓紧时间"有细微差别，其催促的意味会更强一些。

面对突发状况，娴熟传递价值的核心表达

38 客户取消订单，学会应对策略

故事背景

> 香港客户 Mandy 下单后一个多礼拜，突然告知毅冰，因为情况有变，这张订单需要取消。但是生产已经开始，毅冰十分着急，连忙飞去香港跟 Mandy 进行面对面谈判。

Dialogue:

Mandy: Welcome, Yibing! It's great to see you in Hong Kong.

Yibing: Hi, Mandy! Wow, this is a really <u>swanky office</u>!

Mandy: Thanks! How have you been recently?

Yibing: Honestly, things have been <u>a bit chaotic</u>. That's part of why I'm here today.

Mandy: Oh no, Yibing, I'm really sorry to say this, but I have to cancel this order.

Yibing: Wait, what's going on?

Mandy: To be completely transparent with you, our major customer in Mexico is currently facing serious financial trouble. We're hearing whispers of <u>bankruptcy</u>, and we've had to halt all ongoing projects as a precautionary measure.

Yibing: Oh wow, I'm really sorry to hear that. That's a huge blow!

Mandy: It really is.

Yibing: But, Mandy, I need to stress that we're doing business with you, not your customer. We have a signed contract, we've already purchased the raw materials, started mass production, and are on track to ship on time. Regardless of who your end customer is, our contract is with your company, and we've committed significant resources into fulfilling this order. We can't just cancel at this stage—it would put us in a tough spot. I hope you can understand our position.

Mandy: I completely understand. We're actually in the process of reaching out to other clients in Argentina and Brazil to see if they're interested in taking over the goods. I'm currently working on quotes for them, and I'll keep you updated as soon as I have more information.

Yibing: So, does that mean we can move forward with production?

Mandy: Not just yet—everything's on hold for the moment. I'll have a final answer for you by next Wednesday at the latest.

Yibing: Got it. I'll be waiting for your update. <u>The ball's in your court now.</u>

参考译文 📖

Mandy: 欢迎，毅冰！很高兴在香港见到你。

毅冰：嗨，Mandy！哇，这个办公室真是太漂亮了！

Mandy: 谢谢！你最近怎么样？

毅冰：老实说，最近有点混乱。这也是我今天来这里的原因之一。

Mandy: 哦，毅冰，我真的很抱歉，但我不得不取消这笔订单。

毅冰：等等，发生什么事了？

Mandy：说实话，我们在墨西哥的主要客户目前正面临严重的财务问题。我们听到他们即将破产的一些消息，所以不得不暂停所有正在进行的项目，以应对这种情况。

毅冰：哇，我真的很为你们感到抱歉。这确实是个巨大的打击！

Mandy：确实是。

毅冰：但是，Mandy，我必须强调，我们是与你们公司做生意，而不是你们的客户。我们已经签订了合同，购买了原材料，开始进入大规模生产，并且会按时发货。不管你们的最终客户是谁，我们的合同是与你们公司签订的，我们已经投入了大量资源来完成这笔订单。在这个阶段取消订单，对我们来说将会非常困难。我希望您能理解我们的处境。

Mandy：我完全理解。实际上我们正在紧急联系阿根廷和巴西的其他客户，看看他们是否有兴趣接手这些货物。目前我正在为他们做报价，一旦有更多信息，我会立即通知你。

毅冰：那么，我们可以继续生产吗？

Mandy：现在还不行——目前一切都暂时搁置了。我最迟会在下周三，给你一个最终答复。

毅冰：明白了。我会等您的消息。现在就看你们了。

Words & Phrases（词汇和句型）

swanky office 漂亮的办公室

a bit chaotic 乱成一锅粥

bankruptcy 破产

precautionary measure 预防措施

The ball's in your court now! 现在轮到你了！

Chinglish Correction（中式英语纠错）

抱歉我笔误了。船期应该是 1 月 17 日，不是 1 月 7 日。

【Chinglish】

Sorry for my typing mistake. The ship date should be Jan.17th, not 7th.

【Native English】

Sorry for my clerical error. The ship date should be Jan.17th, not 7th.

▶ **毅冰补充：**

"笔误"有一个固定用法 clerical error，在英语国家中很常见。而 typing mistake，很容易听懂，在一些非正式场合也可以使用。但是在正式的口语或书面表达中，如商务谈判之类的，最好用 clerical error。

39　原料价格大涨，引导谈判锚点

故事背景

毅冰跟一俄罗斯客户 Alexandre 讨论下半年的促销订单，可由于原材料大涨的问题，一直在价格上无法谈拢。毅冰建议 Alexandre 根据一年的预期数量一次性下单，但是可以分批出运。这样他就可以安排一次性完成原材料的采购和生产工作，从而限制恒定价格，规避双方的风险。这个建议得到了 Alexandre 的赞同。

Dialogue:

Alexandre: No way, Yibing. This price is 30% higher than your previous quote. That's just crazy!

Yibing: Trust me, I'm going crazy too! The price of raw materials has skyrocketed.

Alexandre: By how much, exactly?

Yibing: It's gone through the roof—about 50% higher than the last time we purchased.

Alexandre: What? So, what are we supposed to do now? Do you think the price will come down anytime soon?

Yibing: Honestly, who knows? I hope it does, but it's hard to predict at this point.

Alexandre: What's your suggestion? We need to place these orders and ship everything within 45 days, or we'll miss the promotion season.

Yibing: I'm feeling the pressure too, trust me. But I think you should go ahead and confirm the new orders right away.

Alexandre: That's easier said than done, Yibing. We've already locked in prices with our customers for a full year. We can't just go back and change the pricing now—it's not an option.

Yibing: Yeah, I see your dilemma. It's a tricky situation for both of us.

Alexandre: Exactly.

Yibing: So, here's what I propose.

Alexandre: I'm all ears.

Yibing: Right now, the cost of raw materials has jumped from 10000 RMB to 15000 RMB. Your last order was based on the 10000 RMB pricing. What if we look at your expected orders for the rest of the year and place them all at once? For instance, you could order 12000 pieces now, 10000 in the next order, and then 20000 later. We could lock in a fixed price for a total of 42000 pieces.

Alexandre: Hmm, what are you getting at?

Yibing: We'd be able to purchase all the raw materials at once and schedule mass production for your full order, but we can still split up the shipments as you need them. This way, we can save on costs and avoid the risk of prices going up even further. And you won't have to worry about the constant price fluctuations for the rest of the year.

Alexandre: That actually sounds like a solid plan. <u>Let's get some skin in the game</u>. I'll need to run this by my director and get approval on the quantities. Send me your best offer for the full lot, and I'll get back to you.

Yibing: Absolutely. I'll have the updated offer ready for you soon.

参考译文 📖

Alexandre：不行，毅冰，这个价格比你之前的报价高出 30%。这简直疯了！

毅冰：相信我，我也快疯了！原材料价格飙升。

Alexandre：究竟涨了多少？

毅冰：涨幅超出预期——比我们上次购买时高了大约 50%。

Alexandre：什么？那我们现在该怎么办？你觉得价格近期会降下来吗？

毅冰：说实话，谁知道呢？我希望它会降，但现在很难预测。

Alexandre：你有什么建议？我们需要在 45 天内下订单并发货，否则就会错过促销季。

毅冰：相信我，我也感受到了压力。但我认为您应该立即确认新订单。

Alexandre：说起来容易做起来难，毅冰。我们已经和客户锁定了一整年的价格。我们不能就这样回去改变定价——这不是一个选择。

毅冰：是的，我理解您的困境。对我们双方来说都是个棘手的情况。

Alexandre：确实如此。

毅冰：所以，我有个提议。

Alexandre：洗耳恭听。

毅冰：现在，原材料的成本已从 10000 元人民币涨到 15000 元人民币。

您上次的订单是基于 10000 元人民币的价格。我们看看您今年剩余的预期订单，如果一次性下所有订单呢？比如，您现在可以订购 12000 件，下次订购 10000 件，之后再订购 20000 件。我们可以为总共 42000 件产品锁定一个固定价格。

Alexandre: 嗯，你的意思是?

毅冰: 我们可以一次性购买所有原材料，并为您的整个订单安排批量生产，但我们仍可以根据您的需求分批发货。这样，我们可以节省成本，并避免价格进一步上涨。今年剩余的时间里您也不必担心价格波动了。

Alexandre: 听起来确实是个不错的计划。让我们也参与进来吧。我需要向我的主管汇报，并确定数量。把你最优惠的报价发给我，我会尽快回复你。

毅冰: 当然，我会尽快更新报价单给你。

Words & Phrases（词汇和句型）

skyrocketed 飞涨、暴涨

predict 预测

That's easier said than done. 说总比做容易。

dilemma 两难处境

Let's get some skin in the game. 让我们也参与进来吧。

Chinglish Correction（中式英语纠错）

Cindy 辞职了? 这太突然了。

【Chinglish】

Does Cindy resign? I'm sorry to hear that.

【Native English】

Cindy quitted? That's out of the blue.

▶ **毅冰补充：**

表示"太突然""十分意外"，口语里可以用 out of the blue，或者 come as a surprise 这样的短语。至于 resign 可以表示辞职，但多为书面语，用于正式的邮件、辞职信等，而 quit 在口语里会更加常用。

40 汇率问题恶化，我们如何应对

故事背景

毅冰的英国客户 David 下了新订单，可毅冰无法接受。因为人民币升值的问题，原有的价格已经没法做了。David 跟毅冰讨论了汇率浮动情况下的恒定价格区间，双方达成共识。

Dialogue:

Yibing: I'm really sorry about this, David, but the updated price is now £2.30 per piece.

David: £2.30? That's way too steep! It's over 5% higher than the last quote.

Yibing: I understand, but it's all down to the revaluation of the RMB. This isn't news to anyone at this point. The reality is, we've actually kept the RMB price the same as before—it's the currency exchange that's driving up the cost.

David: Blimey! That exchange rate's a real kicker.

Yibing: Yeah, I know. But unfortunately, it's something we can't

control.

David: Alright, how about this—you hold the current price for this order, and we can renegotiate the pricing when we place the next one. What do you think?

Yibing: I wish we could, David, but that wouldn't work for us right now. Every supplier in China is grappling with this exchange rate situation. If you were able to pay us in RMB, I could stick to the original price.

David: I'd still have to <u>cough up</u> more pounds to buy the RMB! It doesn't change the issue on my end.

Yibing: You've got a point.

David: What we really need to discuss is setting a pricing window, something valid for a year or two. It'll give us both stability.

Yibing: I get where you're coming from, but that's risky for us. With the way things are looking, the RMB could appreciate even more in the coming years, and I don't think we can afford to sell at a loss.

David: Fair enough. But how about we set a range for the exchange rate fluctuation? Say, within 3%. That way, if the RMB goes up or down within that range, we'll keep the price stable. If it goes up, we take the hit; if it goes down, you pocket the difference, and there's no need for us to ask for a price cut. That way, we both win, right?

Yibing: Hmm, and what happens if the RMB appreciates by more than 3%, say 4%? What do we do then?

David: Simple. We sit down, negotiate again, and agree on a new range. I think that's fair for both sides, don't you?

Yibing: That actually sounds like a pretty good plan. But this is a bit out of my wheelhouse. I'll need to run this by my boss and see what they think.

David: No worries, Yibing. Go ahead and have a chat with your boss, and let me know. I reckon this could work out well for both of us.

参考译文 📖

毅冰： 我真的很抱歉，David，更新后的价格是每件 2.30 英镑。

David： 2.30 英镑？这价格太离谱了！比上次的报价高了 5% 多。

毅冰： 我明白，但这是因为人民币升值。现在大家都知道这个情况。实际上，我们保持了原来的人民币价格不变，真正拉高成本的是汇率。

David： 哎呀！这汇率真让人头疼。

毅冰： 是啊，我知道。但遗憾的是，汇率并不是我们能控制的。

David： 好吧，那这样吧——这次你保持原来的价格，等下次订单时我们再重新谈价格。你觉得怎么样？

毅冰： 我也希望可以这样做，David，但目前我们确实做不到。中国的每一个供应商都在应对这个汇率问题。如果您能用人民币付款，我可以维持原来的价格。

David： 但我还是得用更多的英镑去买人民币！这对我来说问题还是一样的啊。

毅冰： 您说得对。

David： 我们需要讨论的是设定一个价格区间，也许有效期可以是一年或两年。这样我们双方都有稳定性。

毅冰： 我明白您的意思，但对我们来说这有风险。按照目前的情况来看，未来几年人民币可能会进一步升值，我们真的无法承担亏本销售的风险。

David： 有道理。但是我们可以设定一个汇率浮动的范围？比如说，在 3% 以内。这样的话，如果人民币在这个范围内升值或贬值，价格就保持不变。如果人民币升值，我们承担损失；如果贬值，你就能赚到更多，而我们也不要求降价。这样，我们双方都能受益，对吧？

毅冰： 嗯，那如果人民币升值超过 3%，比如 4% 呢？我们该怎么办？

David： 很简单。我们再坐下来谈谈，重新协商一个新的范围。我觉得这样对双方都公平，你觉得呢？

毅冰： 这听起来确实是个不错的方案。不过这有点超出我的权限范围了，我需要跟我的老板汇报一下，看看他们怎么想。

David： 没问题，毅冰。你去和你的老板谈谈，然后告诉我。我觉得这对我们双方来说都会是个不错的解决方案。

Words & Phrases（词汇和句型）

revaluation 贬值

drive up 抬高、上升（一般用于形容成本、价格等）

blimey 哎、天呐（语气词，在英式英语中常见）

real kicker 真正的难题

cough up 被迫付出、被迫交出

Chinglish Correction（中式英语纠错）

抱歉，我有点紧张，请别介意。

【Chinglish】

Sorry, I'm a little nervous. Please don't mind.

【Native English】

Sorry, I have butterflies in my stomach, please don't mind.

▶ **毅冰补充：**

表示"有点紧张"，不一定非要用 nervous。在英语母语国家，本地人口语中经常也会出现一些比喻类的用法。比如，我们形容紧张和忐忑不安，经常会说，"我心里有点儿七上八下"，在英语中可以用 have butterflies in my stomach 来表示。

41 测试碰到麻烦，提出解决方案

故事背景

> 毅冰寄了两次样品给德国客户 Walter，测试机构都指出有问题，在德国检测没有通过。Walter 非常着急，趁着来中国出差，跟毅冰详谈产品的测试问题。

Dialogue:

Yibing: So, I sent you all the CE-EMC, RoHS, SVHC from REACH reports, plus the battery discharge report. That should cover us for the EU market, right?

Walter: Not really, Yibing. I've already submitted your samples to the testing lab twice. The first round didn't go well—we failed on cadmium and PAHs. The results were over the EU limit of 0.1%.

Yibing: I understand. That's why we put together new samples and covered the re-testing fees.

Walter: Yes, and I appreciate that. But unfortunately, we hit another snag.

Yibing: Seriously? We upgraded to a top-quality material for the soft handle, and they assured us it would breeze through the tests.

Walter: We did pass the cadmium and PAHs this time, but the phthalates are still an issue.

Yibing: Ah, that's frustrating!

Walter: I spoke with our engineer in Germany, and he suggested we switch to TPR or silicone gel. In the past, we could pass the 6P phthalates test under the 2005/84/EC regulation, but now we need to comply with the new 17P phthalates standard. It's a big deal for the EU, especially in Germany.

Yibing: Got it, <u>loud and clear</u>. It's a whole new ball game now.

Walter: Exactly. With the <u>surge</u> in claims, the regulations for imports are getting tighter. It's becoming quite a challenge.

Yibing: I totally get that. That's why we're pushing so hard to prepare these samples over and over and absorb those re-testing costs. We really want to win our customers over.

Walter: And I appreciate your effort! It shows commitment.

Yibing: Thanks! If you can give us three days, we'll whip up samples with TPR and silicone handles at lightning speed. How does that sound?

Walter: That sounds perfect! But can we discuss the timeline for future samples? It's crucial we stay ahead of these regulations.

Yibing: Absolutely! Let's set a clear timeline. Maybe we can do a weekly check-in? That way, we can keep everything on track.

Walter: I like that idea. Weekly updates will help us stay aligned, especially with all these changes happening.

Yibing: Great! I'll make sure we have everything ready to roll in three days, and then we can tackle any future adjustments together.

Walter: Sounds like a plan! I'm looking forward to seeing the new samples.

参考译文

毅冰： 我已经把 CE-EMC、RoHS、REACH 的 SVHC 报告和电池放电报告发给你了。这应该足够应对欧盟市场了吧？

Walter： 其实不太够，毅冰。我已经把你的样品提交给检测实验室两次。第一次的结果不太好——我们在镉和多环芳烃上的测试都没达标，结果超过欧盟 0.1% 的限制。

毅冰：我明白了。所以我们准备了新样品，并承担重新测试的费用。

Walter：是的，非常感谢。不过不幸的是，我们又遇到了问题。

毅冰：真的？我们把软把手的材料升级为高质量的材料，他们保证这次能顺利通过测试。

Walter：我们这次通过了镉和多环芳烃的测试，但邻苯二甲酸盐的检测还是没有通过。

毅冰：哎，这太让人沮丧了！

Walter：我跟德国的工程师咨询过，他建议我们换成 TPR 或硅胶。以前，我们的产品可以通过 2005/84/EC 规定的 6P 邻苯二甲酸盐测试，但现在我们必须遵循新的 17P 邻苯二甲酸盐标准。这对欧盟，尤其是德国来说，真的是个大事。

毅冰：明白了。确实是完全不同的局面。

Walter：正是如此。随着投诉的增加，进口产品的法规只会越来越严格。真是个挑战。

毅冰：我完全理解。这就是我们为什么一直在反复准备这些样品并承担重新测试费用的原因。我们真的希望能赢得客户的认可。

Walter：我很感激你们的努力！这体现了你们的承诺。

毅冰：谢谢！如果你能给我们三天时间，我们会以闪电般的速度准备好 TPR 和硅胶把手的样品。你觉得怎么样？

Walter：听起来不错！不过我们能谈谈未来样品的时间安排吗？保持领先于这些规定对我们来说非常重要。

毅冰：当然可以！我们可以制定一个明确的时间表。也许可以每周进行一次检查？这样我们就可以保持一致。

Walter：我喜欢这个主意。每周更新会帮助我们保持同步，尤其是现在变化这么快。

毅冰：太好了！我会确保在三天内准备好所有东西，然后我们可以一起应对未来的变化。

Walter：听起来不错！我期待看到新的样品。

Words & Phrases（词汇和句型）

re-testing fee 重新检测费用

hit another snag 碰到另一个困难

TPR 热塑性橡胶（是一种材料，是 thermoplastic rubber 的简写）

loud and clear 非常清楚

surge 激增、迅速增长

Chinglish Correction（中式英语纠错）

我们会搞定的。

【Chinglish】

We will handle it well.

【Native English】

We will get it done.

▶ **毅冰补充：**

get something done 是固定短语，用来表示搞定问题，解决事情。done 本来就有完成的意思，所以这个表达，比直译的 handle it well 更佳！

42 交期无法赶上，可以这样谈判

故事背景

毅冰经手的一个大订单，因为原材料到位时间推迟，不得已需要延期交货。而这已经超过客户的最后期限，会影响产品上架的时间。毅冰只得跟客户讨论，有没有别的解决办法。

Dialogue:

Yibing: John, I really apologize, but we're going to have to delay two shipments.

John: Yibing, you've got to be kidding me! Can't you push your production team to make sure everything gets shipped on time?

Yibing: I wish it were that simple. The <u>raw materials</u> and parts just arrived two days ago. We need at least 15 days to complete the production run.

John: That's not acceptable. I've already launched the <u>promotional campaign</u>, and the products need to be on our shelves by the beginning of next month.

Yibing: I completely understand. But based on that timeline, we would need to ship next week, and honestly, there's no way we can make that happen.

John: Yibing, this is critical! I need those products by the first week of next month, no exceptions. If you can't meet that, then you'll have to send them via air freight. I can't afford to <u>miss the deadline</u>.

Yibing: John, I know we dropped the ball on the timeline, and

I take full responsibility. But air freight is incredibly costly—it would mean a <u>significant loss</u> on our side. Let me see if we can <u>come up with a compromise</u>.

John: Alright, what's your suggestion?

Yibing: How about this: we can send 15% of the goods by air so you'll have something to sell as planned, and the rest can follow by sea in about two weeks.

John: 15%? That's not going to cut it. I need at least 20% shipped by air, and you'll have to cover the freight charges.

Yibing: Alright, deal. We'll take care of the air freight costs for the 20%. It's on us.

John: Fine. Let's get it done. I'll be expecting those shipments on time.

参考译文 📖

毅冰：John，真的非常抱歉，我们的出货时间要推迟两个船期。

John：毅冰，你是在开玩笑吧！你能不能催一下你的生产部门，确保货物按时发出？

毅冰：我也希望这么简单啊。原材料和配件两天前才到货。我们需要至少 15 天才能完成批量生产。

John：这不行啊。我已经启动了促销活动，产品必须在下个月初上架。

毅冰：我完全理解。但按这个时间算，我们必须在下周发货，而老实说，这根本不可能完成。

John：毅冰，这很关键！不管怎么说，我必须在下个月的第一周收到货物，不能有任何例外。如果你做不到，就给我安排空运，我不能错过这个期限。

毅冰：John，我知道这是我们在订单跟进上的失误，我对此负全部责任。但空运的成本非常高，这会给我们带来巨大的损失。让我来看看我们能不能找到一个折中的解决方案。

John：好吧，你有什么建议？

毅冰：这样吧，我们可以先空运 15% 的货物给你，这样你可以按计划先开始销售，剩下的货物将在两周后通过海运送到。

John：15%？这远远不够。我需要至少 20% 的货物通过空运，而且空运费用得你们承担。

毅冰：好，成交。我们会负责那 20% 的空运费用。这由我们来承担。

John：好。那就这么办。我期待准时收到货物。

Words & Phrases（词汇和句型）

raw material 原材料

promotional campaign 促销活动

miss the deadline 错过截止日期

significant loss 重大损失

come up with a compromise 达成共识

Chinglish Correction（中式英语纠错）

欢迎来我们工厂实地考察。

【Chinglish】

Welcome to visit our factory.

【Native English】

Welcome to conduct a field inspection of our factory.

▶ **毅冰补充：**

英语中，"实地考察"可以用 conduct a field inspection 来表示；visit 就只是拜访、参观，而缺少"考察"的意思。

43 标准谈判，测试要求的精准处理

故事背景

> 毅冰刚完成的一个促销订单在最终验货时出现问题，没有通过检验。客户非常担心，约毅冰在咖啡厅见面，了解具体情况，并商量重验事宜。

Dialogue:

Yibing: Latte or Americano?

Raphael: I think I'll go with my usual <u>Oolong tea</u>. I need something soothing today.

Yibing: Good choice! Can't go wrong with a healthy drink. But I know you're really here to chat about the inspection.

Raphael: Yeah, let's get into that. Honestly, I was pretty shocked. The inspector mentioned that the defects exceeded the <u>AQL</u>, and the shipping marks don't match our specifications.

Yibing: I get it, and it's definitely concerning. But it's not as bad as it sounds. I talked to your inspector yesterday. He was working with an <u>outdated version</u> of the shipping mark. I emailed you the final approved version—should clarify things.

Raphael: I'll check that out tonight. But what about the defects?

Yibing: So, the good news is that all the defects are minor—nothing critical or major. I've already instructed the team to take care of them.

Raphael: What exactly are they doing?

Yibing: They're cleaning up any dust, <u>polishing out</u> the scratches, and then repacking everything. We're on it. I know you'll want to <u>do a re-</u>

inspection, though.

Raphael: Definitely. Can you send me some photos first? I need to reassure my team before we move forward.

Yibing: Absolutely! I'll make sure to get those to you by the end of the day. Is that cool?

Raphael: Perfect. I need to keep everyone in the loop. Our timeline is tight, and delays will be a real headache.

Yibing: Totally understand. We're committed to keeping everything on track. Once you review the photos and give us the thumbs up, I can speed things along on our side.

Raphael: That sounds good. Just keep me posted, okay? Communication is key right now.

Yibing: For sure! We're in this together, and I'll keep you updated every step of the way.

Raphael: Thanks, Yibing. I know it's a lot, but I appreciate your support. We'll get through this.

Yibing: No worries! We've got this. I'll send over those photos ASAP!

参考译文

毅冰：喝拿铁还是美式咖啡？

Raphael：我还是喝我常喝的乌龙茶吧。今天需要点舒缓的饮品。

毅冰：好选择！健康饮料总是不会错。不过我知道你真正想聊的是验货的事。

Raphael：对，咱们聊聊这个。老实说，我有点震惊。检查员说缺陷超出了可接受质量标准，而且唛头与我们的规格不符。

毅冰：我明白，这确实让人担心。但情况并没有听起来那么糟。我昨天跟你的检查员谈过。他拿到的是过时的唛头。我已经把最终批准的版本发给你了——应该能澄清问题。

Raphael：我今晚会看看那个。不过缺陷的情况怎么样？

毅冰：好消息是，所有缺陷都是小问题——没有重大或关键性缺陷。我已经指示团队处理这些问题。

Raphael：他们具体在做什么？

毅冰：他们正在清理灰尘，抛光划痕，然后重新包装一切。我们正在积极处理。我知道你会想要安排重新验货。

Raphael：确实。你能先给我发几张照片吗？我需要让我的团队放心，然后再继续下去。

毅冰：当然可以！我保证今天结束前把照片发给你。这样可以吗？

Raphael：完美。我需要让大家了解情况。时间紧迫，任何延误都会造成麻烦。

毅冰：完全理解。我们会尽力确保一切按计划进行。一旦你审核了照片并给我们确认，我可以加快我们这边的进度。

Raphael：听起来不错。随时保持沟通，没问题吧？现在的关键是沟通。

毅冰：当然！我们是一个团队，我会随时向你更新进展。

Raphael：谢谢你，毅冰。我知道这不容易，但我很感谢你的支持。我们一定能解决这个问题。

毅冰：没问题！我们会搞定的。我会尽快把照片发给你！

Words & Phrases（词汇和句型）

Oolong tea 乌龙茶

AQL 可接受质量标准（acceptable quality level 的首字母缩写）

outdated version 过期版本、过时版本

polish out 抛光

do a re-inspection 安排重新验货

Chinglish Correction（中式英语纠错）

每人来一杯咖啡怎么样?

【Chinglish】

Have a cup of coffee for everybody, ok?

【Native English】

How about a round of coffee?

▶ **毅冰补充:**

a round of 是一个地道的口语表达，表示"每个人都来一杯""每个人都来一份"的意思，如 a round of tea，就是"每人来杯茶"。

更多金句表达，让你随时随地拿出来使用

44 在办公室：畅聊必备的地道英语表达

1) You look exactly the same as last week, still full of energy!

几天不见，你还是那么有活力！

2) Same old, same grind.

还是老样子，忙忙碌碌的。

3) Did you happen to get that email from Michael?

你有没有收到 Michael 的邮件？

4) How about grabbing a coffee?

一起去喝杯咖啡？

5) Could you make sure I get the pricing by the end of today?

确定今天之内给我报价吗？

6) Alright, time to get back to the grind.

好吧，该回去工作了。

7) Where's Lucy? Is she out on maternity leave?

Lucy 呢？她是不是休产假了？

8) What's in it for me in this deal?

我从这笔交易中能得到什么？

9) Could I send you just the photos before the meeting since we're short on time?

会议前我能先发些照片吗？时间有点紧。

10) Don't sweat it, things could be worse.

别纠结，情况可能还会更糟。

11) How's that new project coming along?

那个新项目进展如何了？

12) Are you planning to offer him a better deal?

你打算给他一个更好的报价吗？

13) Thanks a ton! You've really saved the day!

太感谢了！你帮了个大忙！

14) Trust me, I've got this under control.

相信我，我会搞定的。

15) Great job, team! Keep it up!

干得好，大家继续保持！

16) We don't have any samples on hand right now. Could you send us one for review? We'll cover the shipping.

我们手头暂时没有样品。你能寄一个给我们研究吗？我们来付运费。

17) How's everything going over at your company this year?

贵公司今年情况怎么样？

18) I promise, this is our most competitive offer.

我保证，这是我们最具有竞争力的报价。

19) Feel free to take a look around. This is our office area.

随意看看。这里是我们的办公区。

20) We've got a team of 20 here—18 merchandisers and 2 office assistants.

我们这边有 20 个人，其中 18 个跟单，2 个办公室助理。

21) I hope this will open up a new line of communication between us.

我希望这能为我们建立新的沟通渠道。

22) What's your take on the buyer? Do you have a good relationship with them?

你觉得这个买手怎么样？你们关系好吗？

23) I'm pretty new around here, just started a few weeks ago.

我是这里的新人，刚工作几周。

24) Could you put in a good word for us with your higher-ups?

能不能在你们的高层面前帮我们美言几句？

25) Thanks so much for all your help! I really appreciate it.

非常感谢你的帮助！真是太感激了。

26) Let's circle back to this later today, shall we?

我们今天晚些时候再讨论这件事，好吗？

27) Do you have a minute? I need to run something by you.

你有空吗？我有些事想跟你商量一下。

28) Let's touch base on this tomorrow to see where we stand.

明天我们再聊一下，看进展如何。

29) I'm swamped today, can we push this to tomorrow?

我今天特别忙，能把这件事推到明天吗？

30) Could you clarify what you meant by that last point?

你能解释一下刚才提到的那一点吗？

31) Let me loop in the team and we'll get back to you with an update.

我把团队加进来，稍后我们会给你最新情况。

32) Let's take this offline and discuss it further.

我们私下再详细讨论这个问题吧。

33) I'll make sure this gets on the agenda for our next meeting.

我保证这个问题会列入我们下次会议的议程。

34) It's been a pleasure working with you on this project!

很高兴跟你一起合作这个项目！

35) Let's prioritize this task so we can meet the deadline.

我们优先处理这项任务，以确保赶上截止日期。

36) Do you have any bandwidth to help out with this project?

你还有时间参与这个项目吗？

37) That's a great idea, let's run with it.

这是个好主意，我们就照这个思路做。

38) Let's sync up later and make sure we're on the same page.

我们稍后再沟通一下，确保我们步调一致。

39) Can you give me a quick rundown of the main points?

你能快速给我讲一下要点吗？

40) I really appreciate your attention to detail on this.

我非常感谢你对这件事的细心关注。

45 在工厂里：轻松接待客户和现场走访

41) Hi Andy, it's great to have you here at our factory!

Andy，很高兴你来我们工厂参观！

42) How's everything going today? Feeling good?

今天感觉如何？一切顺利吗？

43) Right this way, please!

请这边走！

44) This is our production workshop. As you can see, we've got four injection machines and two printing machines here.

这里是我们的生产车间。你可以看到，我们有4台注塑机和2台印刷机。

45) We're a family-owned business with over 10 years of experience in this industry.

我们是一家家族企业，在这个行业已经有超过10年的经验。

46) We have more than 200 skilled workers on staff, which is a major advantage for us.

我们有 200 多名熟练工人，这是我们的一大优势。

47) The restroom? Sure, follow him, he'll show you the way.

洗手间？当然，跟着他，他会带你去的。

48) This is our assembly workshop, where we focus on assembling and debugging products.

这是我们的装配车间，主要负责产品的组装和调试。

49) We've always been at the forefront of this industry.

我们一直走在这个行业的前沿。

50) I can assure you, every piece is tested twice before it's shipped out.

我可以向你保证，每个产品出货前都会经过两次测试。

51) It's a cakewalk for us.

这对我们来说易如反掌。

52) That's ok. No sweat.

没事儿。举手之劳。

53) We take pride in producing a wide range of patented products.

我们非常自豪能够生产多种自有专利产品。

54) Here's our latest model for the upcoming season. Feel free to give it a try!

这是我们为下个季节开发的新品。欢迎试用！

55) We primarily supply products to importers in the US.

我们主要给美国进口商供货。

56) I'm not entirely sure who the final retailer is.

我不太确定谁是最终的零售商。

57) Jack is our sales representative in the US. From now on, he'll be your direct point of contact.

Jack 是我们在美国的销售代表。接下来他会直接与你联系。

58) Our warehouse is more than big enough to handle large orders.

我们的仓库足够大，可以应对大订单。

59) Sorry, but no photos are allowed in the production area.

不好意思，生产区域内禁止拍照。

60) Let me show you around the factory. You'll get a sense of how everything works here.

我带你参观一下工厂。你可以了解一下我们这里的运作方式。

61) Our team has extensive experience in manufacturing, which allows us to deliver top-quality products.

我们的团队拥有丰富的制造经验，可以确保我们能够提供高质量的产品。

62) This section is where we handle quality control. Each product is thoroughly inspected before shipping.

这里是我们进行品控的区域。每件产品在发货前都会进行严格检查。

63) We're currently investing in new technologies to further improve our production efficiency.

我们正在投资新技术，从而进一步提高生产效率。

64) Our factory operates 24/7, so we're able to meet tight deadlines.

我们的工厂全天候运作，能够应对紧迫的交货期。

65) We can customize the packaging according to your specifications.

我们可以根据您的要求定制包装。

66) Let me introduce you to our head of production, he oversees the entire manufacturing process.

我给您介绍一下我们的生产主管，他负责整个生产过程。

67) Our assembly line is highly automated, which helps us maintain consistent quality.

我们的装配线高度自动化，有助于保持品质的稳定。

68) We work with some of the largest retailers in the US, including Walmart and Target.

我们与美国一些大零售商有合作，包括沃尔玛和塔吉特。

69) We're constantly innovating to stay ahead of the competition.

我们不断创新，以保持竞争优势。

70) We've implemented a strict quality management system to ensure that every product meets our high standards.

我们实施严格的质量管理体系，以确保每个产品都符合我们的高标准。

71) Our production capacity allows us to handle both small and large-scale orders.

我们的生产能力可以处理小批量和大批量订单。

72) We're proud of the long-term partnerships we've built with our clients over the years.

我们为多年来与客户建立的长期合作关系感到自豪。

73) We can work together to develop customized solutions that meet your specific needs.

我们可以合作开发符合您具体需求的定制解决方案。

74) Our follow-up team is very efficient, ensuring that your products are delivered on time.

我们的物流团队非常高效，可以保证您的产品按时交付。

75) Thank you for visiting today. We hope this tour has given you a good understanding of our capabilities.

感谢您今天的参观。希望这次参观让您对我们的能力有更深入的了解。

46 在样品间：这些都是我压箱底的金句

76) Hey guys, what would you prefer? Coke or Evian?

各位，想喝点什么？可乐还是依云水？

77) How's everything going?

最近怎么样？

78) Sorry, this product's locked down for New Zealand market—contract rules.

抱歉，这个产品我们在新西兰市场有合约，无法销售。

79) What if we tried it out in Scandinavia instead?

我们不如试试北欧市场怎么样？

80) Europe's our main market—Germany, the UK, and the whole Benelux region.

我们的主要市场在欧洲，特别是德国、英国，还有比荷卢三国。

81) Our stuff's cleared all the tests in France, so you're all good there.

我们的产品已经通过了法国所有的测试，完全没问题。

82) Wanna team up on this one?

有兴趣一起合作这个项目吗？

83) We're keeping the new stuff under wraps for now—you'll only see it here.

我们的新品还没有公开展示，只能在这里看到。

84) We've got some fresh designs lined up. Check them out.

我们准备了一些新款。来看看吧。

85) I'll shoot you the price list tonight.

我今晚把报价单发给你。

86) Sorry, that's a patented item, but we've got a similar version you'll like.

抱歉，这款有专利，不过我们有类似款，你肯定喜欢。

87) No problem, we can totally do OEM for you.

没问题，贴牌我们完全可以搞定。

88) I snapped photos and made notes—I'll send you the updated sample soon.

我拍了照片，记下了要点，很快会给你寄新样品。

89) Here's my card. Hit me up if you need anything.

这是我的名片。有事随时联系。

90) I'd skip this packaging if I were you—it's crazy expensive.

如果是我的话，不会选这个包装，这实在贵得离谱。

91) Let me give you a quick heads-up on what we've got.

让我简短介绍一下我们都有哪些产品。

92) We know you've got a ton of stores across Central and Western Europe.

我们知道你们在中西欧有很多门店。

93) I'll be in the US this fall—I'll bring you some of our new releases then.

我今年秋天要去美国，到时给你带点我们的新品看看。

94) We've been in this game for over 10 years now. Family business.

我们在这行干了超过 10 年，家族企业。

95) Want to grab a coffee before we get started?

开工前要不要先喝杯咖啡？

96) Feel free to browse, and if anything catches your eye, just tell me.

随便看看，有兴趣的产品告诉我就行。

97) We can adjust the MOQ to accommodate your needs.

我们可以调整最小起订量以满足您的需求。

98) We can produce this under the Disney brand, but we'll need to see the official authorization letter first.

我们可以用迪士尼品牌生产这个产品，但需要先看到官方授权书。

99) Take a look at this one. It's been super popular with our clients lately.

来看看这款吧。最近客户们特别喜欢。

100) We can tweak the color or finish if you need something more custom.

如果您需要定制，我们可以调整颜色或者进行表面处理。

47　在谈判桌：核心内容与商业智慧并存

101) We really can't go any lower on price. Hope you understand.

我们没法再降价了。请您理解。

102) No, that's over our budget. Can we bring it down a bit?

不行啊，这超过我们预算了。能把价格稍微降一点吗？

103) Any chance we can ship this as a partial load?

我们能不能安排分批出货？

104) Our minimum order is one full 40-foot container.

我们的最小订单是基于一个 40 尺柜的数量。

105) Honestly, we feel let down. This is only 10% of what you promised.

坦白说，我们感觉不太好。这里只有你当初承诺数量的十分之一。

106) Let me check with BV about the testing fees and get back to you.

让我们跟 BV 公司确认一下测试费用，会尽快答复您的。

107) Nope, it's FOB terms, not CIF.

不是的，这个价格是离岸价，不是到岸价。

108) They only handle the paperwork for us, nothing else.

他们只是给我们做一些文书工作，并没有其他。

109) I'll FedEx the samples to you in 3 days, tops.

三天内我会用联邦快递给您寄样品。

110) We have to negotiate the price again, because of the raw material price pressure.

由于原材料价格的上涨，我们需要重新谈一下价格。

111) Please make sure that you can settle the payment as quickly as possible.

请确认您会尽快安排货款。

112) Sure, we could accept L/C at sight or T/T at sight.

当然，我们可以接受即期信用证或即期电汇转账。

113) A 10% discount? No way we can do that.

10% 的折扣？我们完全办不到。

114) We can hook you up with door-to-door delivery.

我们可以给你安排门到门的服务。

115) Got it. Can you share your courier account with us?

明白。能否发我一下你的快递到付账号？

116) That's the net price, doesn't include testing or sampling fees.

那个仅仅是产品的净价，不包含测试费和打样费。

117) Applying for the GS cert is too pricey on our end. Please go ahead by your side.

申请 GS 认证实在太贵了。你们可以自行安排。

118) Deal! A trial order for 500pcs.

成交！我们从 500 件的小订单开始吧。

119) Which port are we shipping to? Long Beach in the US?

目的港在哪里？美国长滩港吗？

120) Our packaging's solid, it'll definitely pass the drop test.

我们的包装足够结实，完全可以通过摔箱跌落测试。

121) Your QC can swing by for an inspection next week, if that works.

如果可以的话，你们的验货员下周可以来验货了。

122) Our price is pretty reasonable.

我们的价格十分合理。

123) It is amazing if our pricing is far more expensive than others, make sure you're comparing apples to apples.

我们的价格远高于同行是不现实的，请确信我们的产品完全一致。

124) We're bringing in a third party to manage after-sales service in the US.

我们会安排一个第三方公司来处理我们产品在美国的售后服务。

125) Can we work out a payment schedule that suits both sides?

我们能否商量一个彼此能接受的付款方式？

126) This is the best offer we can do—anything lower, and we're taking a loss.

这是我们能做的最低价格了，再低就亏本。

127) We've streamlined production to meet tighter deadlines.

我们已经优化了生产流程，可以应对更紧急的交货要求。

128) Let's keep it simple—what's the main sticking point for you?

直说吧，主要问题是什么？

129) We'll need at least 30 days for production after we get the green light.

在收到客户确认后，我们至少需要 30 天来完成生产。

130) Let's clarify the shipping terms so there's no confusion later.

我们先把运输条款弄清楚，这样后续不容易产生误会。

131) Our competitors are cutting corners—we're not doing that.

我们的同行在偷工减料，我们不会那样做。

132) Can you give me a rough timeline for when you need the first batch?

您能给我一个大概的时间表，什么时候需要第一批货吗？

133) Our current capacity is maxed out, but we can ramp up if needed.

目前我们的产能已经饱和，但如果有需要我们还能扩充。

134) Let's set up a video call to iron out the details.

让我们安排一个视频会议来敲定相关细节吧。

135) We've already factored in your concerns about packaging costs.

我们已经考虑到您对包装成本的担忧。

48 在闲聊时：用地道母语思维拉近距离

136) Alright, see you tomorrow at 8 a.m. in the lobby.

好的，明早八点酒店大堂见。

137) How'd you manage to score such a good deal?

您是怎么拿到这么好的折扣？

138) Man, hotel prices during the HK Fair are insane!

大哥，香港展期间的酒店价格涨疯了！

139) I gotta head out.

我得走了。

140) I'm heading to the US for vacation next month.

我下个月要去美国度假。

141) Don't flake on me!

别放我鸽子啊！

142) I'm driving home, I'll call you back in like 10 minutes.

我在开车回家的路上，10分钟后给你打回去。

143) Is it tough to get a Schengen Visa?

申根签证难申请吗？

144) So, I'm guessing you're not getting much sleep on this trip?

我想，这次行程您一定没休息好吧？

145) Thanks for inviting me to dinner. Any dress code I should know about?

感谢您邀请我参加晚宴。着装上有什么特别要注意的吗？

146) Yeah, I'm pretty much on the same page with you.

是呢，我基本同意您的观点。

147) I'm gonna hit the shower first. See you at the coffee bar.

我先去冲个澡。一会儿咖啡厅见。

148) Just being asked is an honor.

能问我，这就已经是我的荣幸了。

149) Buckle up, please.

请系好安全带。

150) So, how's the jet lag treating you?

倒时差怎么样？还习惯吗？

151) Are you into any good shows lately?

最近有追什么好剧吗？

152) You gotta try the local street food, it's the best!

您一定得尝尝这里的街头小吃，超棒的！

153) Catch you later! Don't be a stranger!

回头见！别失联啊！

154) We should grab a drink after the meeting.

会议结束后我们去喝一杯吧。

155) Did you get a chance to check out the city?

您有时间逛逛这座城市吗？

156) That restaurant you suggested. Total game-changer!

你推荐的那家餐厅，简直神了！

157) What do you do to unwind after a long day?

忙完一天您会怎么放松？

158) I've got a killer spot for brunch tomorrow if you're free.

要是您明天有空，我带您去一家超棒的早午餐店。

159) Any big plans after this business trip?

这次出差后，有什么大计划吗？

160) I swear, every time I'm here, I put on 1 kilogram from all the food!

我发誓，我每次来这里吃饭吃到扶墙出，回去都要胖两斤。

161) Man, I could really go for a coffee right now.

天呐，我现在真想来杯咖啡。

162) Can't believe how fast this week's flown by!

真不敢相信这周过得这么快！

163) Next time you're in town, I'll show you around.

下次您来，我带您四处走走。

164) What's the next stop on your travel list?

接下来准备去哪里旅行？

165) If you're free tonight, let's hit up that new rooftop bar.

今晚有空的话，去试试那家新开的屋顶酒吧。

49 在就餐时：学老外餐桌上的热门话题

166) Table for two, non-smoking, please.

麻烦给我们安排一个两人位，无烟区，谢谢！

167) I got this one!

这次我请客！

168) Bill, please!

买单！

169) This food looks amazing. My mouth's watering already.

这菜看起来太棒了。我都要流口水了。

170) Wanna try some local dishes?

想不想试试本地菜？

171) Can we order now?

我们能点菜了吗？

172) No, we'll split the bill.

不用了，帮我们分开账单支付吧。

173) Still or sparkling water?

要纯净水还是气泡水？

174) Hey Michael, how about we grab some Peking Duck?

Michael，我们去吃北京烤鸭怎么样？

175) The dim sum here are seriously good!

这儿的点心真是太好吃了！

176) Can I get a toffee nut latte with extra cream, please?

给我来杯太妃榛果拿铁，加双份奶油。

177) The braised crab with vermicelli is a must-try here.

这儿的螃蟹粉丝煲绝对不能错过。

178) How do you like your steak cooked?

牛排要几分熟?

179) Go easy on the salt and no MSG, please.

麻烦少加点盐，别放味精。

180) We're thinking something lighter for tonight.

我们今晚考虑来点轻食。

181) I'll handle the ordering this time.

这次我来点菜吧。

182) This food is totally my jam.

这些菜太对我胃口了。

183) Can we get a couple of appetizers to start?

我们先来点开胃菜吧?

184) What's your go-to drink when you're out?

你平时吃饭都喝点什么?

185) Let's get the house special. I've heard it's amazing.

我们点这里的招牌菜吧。听说很不错。

186) You've gotta try this, it's my favorite dish here.

你得尝尝这个，这是我在这家店最喜欢的菜。

187) I'm thinking about getting the seafood platter, you in?

我打算点个海鲜拼盘，你一起来点？

188) This wine pairs perfectly with the steak.

这款酒和牛排简直是绝配。

189) I'm so full, but I could still go for some dessert.

我饱了，但还有胃口吃甜品。

190) You should definitely try the fried dumplings, they're a hit here.

你一定得试试这儿的煎饺，超级受欢迎。

191) You're gonna love this place. It's my go-to spot.

你一定会喜欢这里的。这可是我常来的地方。

192) We should totally come back here next time.

下次我们一定再来这里。

193) This sauce is incredible, it really makes the dish.

这酱汁绝了，整道菜就靠它了。

194) How about we split a pizza? Half and half?

要不我们点个披萨，分着吃？

195) Do you want to order another round of drinks?

要不再来一轮喝的吧？

50 在电话中：告别尴尬的事先"小抄"准备

196) Hey, it's Cindy on the line.

嗨，我是 Cindy。

197) Sorry to bother you so late!

抱歉这么晚打扰你！

198) Could I talk to Jennifer, please?

请问 Jennifer 在吗？

199) Oops, I think I have the wrong number.

汗，我打错电话了。

200) Sorry, I can't catch that. Could you repeat it?

抱歉，我没听清。能再说一遍吗？

201) Do you know when he'll be back?

你知道他什么时候回来吗？

202) Could you pass along a message for me?

能帮我转告一下吗？

203) Hi there, is Vincent around?

你好，请问 Vincent 在吗？

204) I'm sorry, but he's in Frankfurt on a business trip.

抱歉，他去法兰克福出差了。

205) Yes, please hold for a moment.

是的，请稍等一下。

206) Alright, I'll try his cell.

好的，我会打他手机的。

207) He's not here right now. Want to try again in half an hour?

他现在不在。要不你半小时后再打来？

208) I'm calling to see how the samples are doing.

我打这个电话是想了解一下样品的进展。

209) We have a lot of Mikes here. Can you tell me the last name?

我们这儿有很多叫 Mike 的，请告诉我你要找的 Mike 姓什么？

210) Can you share your email address with me?

能告诉我你的邮箱地址吗？

211) Could you jot down my email address, please?

能麻烦你记一下我的邮箱地址吗？

212) That's all for now, thanks! I should get going.

就这些，谢谢你！我得挂了。

213) Great chatting with you!

跟你聊得很愉快！

214) Would it be cool to visit your office next Monday?

下周一我方便来你们公司拜访吗？

215) Are you free to chat for a bit?

你现在有空聊一会儿吗？

216) Just checking in about our last conversation.

我只是想跟进一下我们上次的谈话。

217) Can you hold on while I grab a pen?

能稍等一下吗？我去拿支笔。

218) Thanks for taking the time to talk!

感谢你抽时间跟我通话！

219) I'll email you the details after our call.

我会在电话后，把详情发你邮件。

220) Is it alright if I call you back in a bit?

稍后再给你打回去可以吗？

221) I'll make sure to keep you in the loop.

我保证，会让你随时了解情况进展。

222) I'll look into that and get back to you.

我会调查一下，然后再回复你。